"Many who would like to live in an interactive walk with God cannot find their way to it because they simply do not know what to do. The details defeat them. *Whispers* provides clear and simple instructions on entering and abiding in real life interaction with God. You only need do what the book says and the reality of eternal living will validate itself in your experience. What one sees in the Bible and in the lives of the "great ones" in the way of Christ will progressively become how you actually go through your day-to-day journey in the Kingdom of God."

DALLAS WILLARD
Author of *Hearing God* and *The Divine Conspiracy*

"Looking at the Grand Canyon we get the feeling that something really powerful has been at work. Rarely can we tell that the little stream at the bottom is that 'powerful force.' *Whispers of My Abba* can only be described as powerful like the Colorado River. But unlike the Colorado it is also wonderfully clear. David Takle has laid out his teaching in a 'three pass' approach that lets us begin immediately on the first pass, go deeper on the second, and solve problems on the third pass. This is a book for people whose attempts to listen to God have not been working, as David addresses common problems and helps us learn from our attempts to connect with God. This book is not for those who want to argue about listening to God, but instead provides a gentle path to those who are ready to try."

JIM WILDER
Author, and director of Shepherd's House
Pasadena, CA.

"In *Whispers of my Abba*, David Takle has let us in on his own experience of prayer in a way that makes that divine–human dialogue appealing and accessible for those who are just beginning to get to know our communicating God, and takes those who have been in that space already to an even deeper place."

KEITH MEYER
Coach of pastors and author of
Whole Life Transformation: Becoming The Change Your Church Needs

"From the Garden onward God has sought to connect with mankind. In his new book David Takle envisions this relational connection happening through natural conversations between us and our Maker. Using practical illustrations and helpful insights gained from actual shared moments with God, the author moves the reader into realizing that we, too, are meant to meet and converse with the One who seeks us. Takle provides a fresh and liberating approach to knowing God by mentoring readers in these occasions. As the participants become aware of how fulfilling and transforming such encounters can be and how invitingly simple Takle makes the process of hearing, they will be tempted to experience being conversational partners with God and in so doing discover new intimacy, new perspectives on God and new persons they are becoming in these encounters."

DR. JULIE GORMAN
Professor of Christian Formation and Discipleship
Fuller Seminary, Pasadena, CA.

"David Takle has done all of us a great service in *Whispers of my Abba*. He has helped restore the life-giving reality of hearing God's voice to every follower of Jesus. This book is personal and practical and will be a great help to those who read it."

STEVE SUMMERELL
Pastor and spiritual director

Whispers of my Abba

From His Heart to Mine

by David Takle, M.Div.

Whispers of my Abba

is available from

Resources.LifeModel.org
and
Amazon.com

Whispers of my Abba
ISBN-10: 1-935629-04-2
ISBN-13: 978-1-935629-04-7
Published by Shepherd's House, Inc.
P.O. Box 40096
Pasadena, CA 91114
www.LifeModel.org

Unless otherwise noted, all Scripture references are taken from the New International Version of the Bible (Zondervan: Grand Rapids) 1996

For all my grandchildren:

May God always be your constant companion

Whispers of my Abba

Table of Contents

Acknowledgments

Learning to have conversations with God was not something I set out to discover on my own. It was something God brought into my life over time through the ministry of others. There are three people in particular I would like to thank here for the contributions they made toward this particular aspect of my journey.

First, Ned Berube, who taught me about spiritual reflection as an immensely valuable process in and of itself. Then Ed Smith, who pointed the way toward hearing God speak directly into my life. And finally, Mark Virkler, who showed me that conversations with God are meant to be part of our normal Christian experience.

Of course the gifts do not end there. By the grace of God, the book that is in your hands now is very different from the one I originally wrote. I am deeply indebted to all those who read the manuscript and provided the many corrections and critiques necessary to make this book more readable. Especially significant to me has been the thoughtfulness and insightful feedback of my wife, Jan, whose encouragement to me throughout this project has been invaluable.

Thank you, Lord, for giving me all that made this book possible.
And may it be a gift as well to all who read it.

Preface

I have been a Christian for nearly fifty-five years, much of that time very actively involved in churches that were fairly serious about trying to live out the gospel in today's world. I studied theology, taught classes, led small groups, and memorized Scripture. In the process, I learned a lot about what is helpful and what brings life. But without a doubt, the single most valuable thing I have learned is this: *How to have conversations with God.*

That might sound surprising to some. If you were to go by what most of us were taught about the Christian life, you would never know how incredibly important this is. You might not even know that it is possible. But the truth is that God *loves* to speak to his children. He longs to teach us about himself, to comfort us when we need comfort, to speak into our broken places and dispel the darkness, to feed our soul and quench our thirst. Learning how to listen to the Spirit of God and engage with him is like discovering Narnia behind the wardrobe (Lewis). An entirely new world becomes accessible to us – one that previously we could only wish might be real.

God alone can speak life into existence. And that life becomes life in me as I learn how to hear God speak into *my* life.

I am writing this book for those who want to hear God's voice, and want to hear it with more clarity and with more confidence than they have ever had before. I know there are some who may think this is too good to be true, and even some who are sure this is not possible at all. Although I have included sufficient evidence from Scripture to show that God does in fact speak to each of us personally, I do not intend to try and convince anyone that this is true. If you need help believing that God still speaks today, I recommend Dallas Willard's book *Hearing God* where he has done an excellent job of presenting a sound theological basis for engaging with God in two-way conversational prayer. I cannot improve on what he has done there.

My hope for this present work is to help Christians who long to hear their Papa's voice more clearly, who desire to engage with the Spirit of God as a Mentor for life, who want more help in how to listen and what to listen for, and who want to know how to make space for this kind of interaction with God. I invite you to join me on a journey that may well change forever your relationship to God, a journey that will open the doors to the Kingdom that Jesus made possible.

In every place where these things have been taught, we have seen life spring up before our eyes and God's people renewed, overjoyed at how amazing their relationship with God becomes when they can hear him and have real conversations with him. We were never meant to live the Christian life by our own wits or by an education in doctrine and ethics alone. It is only when we learn how to engage with God in conversation that we have any real hope for ongoing, life-long transformation and renewal.

> "A time is coming and has now come when the dead will hear the voice of the Son of God and those who hear will live." (Jn.5:25)

This is Jesus' promise to us. Let us seek him and learn how to hear him and live by his words.

– David Takle

A Note About Gender Inclusiveness

Due to the limitations of our language, every English author has to decide how to address the issue of inclusiveness regarding gender when using pronouns. Reading the phrase "he or she" all the time is very cumbersome, using only "he" *or* "she" sounds very biased in modern literature, and randomly switching between the two is often disorienting.

One solution is to refer to "you" all the time, but that generally comes across as too preachy. Another approach is to use "I" and "my," but after a while that begins to sound a little egotistical.

Consequently, I have opted for the convention of using an inclusive plural, despite the fact that this results in grammatically incorrect sentences, mixing singular and plural words quite loosely. So instead of:

> "When a person sets aside time to be with God, he or she needs to quiet his or her mind and focus his or her heart."

I will tend to use:

> "When we set aside time to be with God, we need to quiet our mind and focus our heart."

My assumption is that since we hear this kind of grammar all the time, and since I intend to be fairly informal in this book anyway, most readers will have little trouble with the license I have taken with the language. I hope you will find this to be an acceptable solution.

Part 1 – Getting Started

My prayer for you is that these first four chapters would provide enough of a start that your prayer life will never be the same. I have tried to be as succinct as possible, and at the same time include enough to be clear about what it is like to have two-way conversations with God.

Chapter 1 – Conversations with God?

What does conversational prayer look like? What is its purpose? Can we really trust it?

Chapter 2 – Listening in on Real Conversations

A collection of real conversations with God that have been drawn from personal journals, with additional notations to help explain what is going on in the mind and heart of the writer.

Chapter 3 – Four Aspects of Conversations with God

Conversational prayer described as an interweaving of Focusing, Listening, Discerning, and Responding.

Chapter 4 – How Writing Can Help

How writing out our conversations with God can significantly improve our ability to hear and discern more clearly.

Chapter 1 – Conversations with God?

"It is written in the prophets, 'And they shall all be taught by God.' Everyone who has heard and learned from the Father comes to me" (Jn.6:45).

Does Jesus mean we will have *actual real live conversations* with God? Like when he taught his disciples? As in ... we could talk to him and he would talk to us?

Oh, Yes!

And more!

Is Jesus talking about hearing voices in our head?

No, he is not encouraging a fantasy life. God designed us to engage with him, and we can learn how.

Does God speak in an audible voice?

God rarely speaks to us audibly, although it is not uncommon for us to receive fully formed thoughts in our mind that flow easily into sentences. God's voice is generally more subtle. But we can learn to tell the difference between his voice and our own.

What if I'm not sure I want to hear what he has to say? Wouldn't he just tell me all the things I'm doing wrong or how disappointed he is in me?

He's really not like that. You would be pleasantly surprised how much God loves you and how much he wants to spend time with you and help you, not condemn you.

Could he explain to me why my life is such a mess? Can he help me where I'm feeling stuck?

One of God's deepest desires is to set you free and mentor you so that you can become the person he created you to be.

Don't we need to have some sort of spiritual gift or have someone lay hands on us or something?

No. All we need to do is to make time for God and learn how to have conversations with him.

How do we begin? When can we start?

Right now. Join me as we take this journey together and discover our birthright as God's beloved children.

A GENTLE WHISPER

Listening to God can be a little hard to describe, since he can speak to us in so many different ways. Perhaps if I share with you an entry from my own journal, you can begin to get a better picture of what this might look like. The following conversation took place one day when I was contemplating a morsel from Psalm 23.

"You prepare a table before me ... you anoint my head with oil; my cup overflows" (Ps.23:5).

As I reflect on this image, Lord, I see a table spread for a feast. Food everywhere. Platters overflowing with rich food.

But the thing that has my attention today is the cup – a large silver cup overflowing with wine. Rich, purple wine. This picture really stirs my heart – I don't know why.

Why is it "overflowing" anyway?

It can only mean "abundance." This is not wine that is scarce, or wine that I have to earn, but wine in abundance, overflowing, more than I can ever taste, let alone drink.

[I pause here, allowing myself to feel the immense abundance represented by this image. An insight dawns on me.]

The cup in my picture is bubbling up from inside and overflowing very much like a fountain.

This is not how a cup overflows! A cup overflows when someone is pouring into it and not stopping.

[In my mind's eye, I back away from the image so I can see Jesus pouring into the cup. As I do so, I see him thoroughly enjoying himself as he pours the wine and watches it flow all over the table. He has so much to give that he keeps pouring without any regard for the extravagant "waste."]

What an amazing image!

I've got to get a bigger cup!

You have so much love to give!

Your generosity is outrageous – radical – infinite. You give me more than I can ever receive and enough to give away without ever running dry.

I am overwhelmed by your goodness, your generous desire to pour into me far beyond all that I can imagine or receive. Relieve my doubts, my belief in scarcity, my scavenger mentality. Forgive me for making you out to be stingy or someone from whom I need to beg for what I need.

Help me receive! Give me a receiving heart. Give me what I need, in order to receive more of what you have to give.

I see myself now standing under a waterfall, eyes closed, feeling the refreshing water pour down on my soul.

I believe. I receive.

I think I'll just stay here for a while and let you pour into my heart. In Jesus' name ... Thank you, Lord.

A Relationship that Changes Everything

Imagine what it would be like to have a relationship with someone who knows you completely, everything about you from the inside out, and totally loves you at the same time! Now imagine this person has an incredible heart, is kinder than anyone you have ever known, cares deeply for your soul, and has so much wisdom that you are totally captivated every time he speaks.

Add to this his total availability and the absolute certainty that he will never leave you, never abandon you, never trick you or betray you. He is completely trustworthy and utterly faithful. Without a doubt, he is the best friend you could ever have. And he wants to help you in ways that no one else even knows how to.

You also know that he is no pushover. He knows all about the flaws and holes in your life and has no intention of leaving them untouched. When you sit down to talk with him about one of these areas, he shows you what is in your heart that needs renewing. But he does so in a way that is so graceful, so loving and so freeing, you know he holds you in his heart and has only your best interest in mind. His gentle way of addressing even hard things is more of a gift than a correction, largely because he knows exactly what you need for the renewal you desire. And when your conversation is over, you are far less encumbered, more at peace, and grateful for his guiding light in your life.

Sound good? Perhaps too good to be true?

This is but a taste of what a relationship with God can be – an authentic, vibrant, life-giving relationship that goes way beyond what many Christians have ever known. And when we say "relationship" we are not talking about some legal standing with God that we inherited at our conversion, but a practical, tangible, experiential relationship in which we have direct access to God. And this includes having conversations with him that breathe life and goodness into our soul, changing us day by day to become more like Christ, and filling our heart with more joy than we could ever have the capacity to receive.

In my own life, conversations with God have encouraged me when I was down, provided guidance in confusing places, given me hope when I felt hopeless, healed much of my broken soul, and helped me to become more the person he meant me to be. Most of all, these conversations have become the cornerstone of a relationship that I did not even know was possible. I can scarcely imagine where I would be today if I had not learned how to hear him and have conversations with him.

To put this all in a single statement: *Conversational prayer is the means by which we can engage with God at the deepest levels of our soul and receive his words of life directly into our heart and mind.*

This is how we were meant to live!

AN OVERVIEW OF CONVERSATIONAL PRAYER

Allow me to shift gears for a few minutes and give you a bird's eye view of conversational prayer. Let's begin by making a few comparisons between the kinds of conversations we have with God and those we normally have with people.

In deep conversations with others we are close to, we share our heart, listen to what they say and how they say it, the reasons behind what they are saying, what they leave unsaid, and the way in which they are emotionally present with us. In short, we listen on multiple levels – paying attention to the content of what is being said as well as the context and manner of our conversation. These are all part of how we make sense of our interaction with them.

Listening to God is similar in that we must learn to pay attention on several levels at once. And as with other people we care about, our love for God and our desire to nurture our relationship with him are essential elements that lend focus and purpose to our conversations.

Where it is dissimilar from human communication is that God's way of speaking to us is usually inaudible and comes to us primarily as impressions, words and images. The Bible tells us that God's Spirit and our spirit are able to communicate with each another very directly (Rom.8:16; 1Cor.2:13-14). With guidance, practice and patience, most of us can learn how to receive and understand what God is revealing to us. And the evidence that this is all true can be seen in the over-abundance of fruit that results from hearing him speak into our life, not to mention the many promises we have in Scripture that say we would be able to know his voice.

Perhaps the most surprising thing of all is that the actual effort of hearing God can be much less than we might imagine. In fact, the simplicity of it can almost be a stumbling block because we tend to think that if it were that simple we would already know how to do it.

But this is just one of many ways in which the Kingdom of God is at odds with our earthly way of seeing things. Much of our practical knowledge of spiritual things can be upside down, even if we know a lot of theology. One very important thing we want to turn right-side up is the understanding that hearing from God does not require any special spiritual gift reserved only for prophets or other uniquely gifted people. Talking with God is not only non-sensational, for the most part it is not even dependent upon how well we think we are doing spiritually. God wants to speak to us no matter how messed up we are or how well we may be doing at the moment.

Perhaps we should add this one qualifier: *if we really have no intention of being changed by our relationship with God, then it is*

unlikely that we will be able to hear him very well or discern his voice.
Spiritual discernment does not come easily to those who have no
desire to be involved in the life of Christ. We can, of course, ask
for that desire to be birthed in us by the Holy Spirit and ask to be
changed by him.

The point is that conversational prayer is *normal.* God designed
us to be able to communicate with him, and he places in our heart
the desire to do so. All we need to do is learn how, and begin to
engage with him.

The Four Aspects of Conversational Prayer

Given that we want to develop a conversational prayer life with
God that is both reliable and good for our soul, we need to break
this down and look at the various elements of what we are actually
involved in during our time with God.

Conversational prayer lends itself quite nicely to being viewed
as a combination of four inter-connected processes that we engage
in to varying degrees at any moment during our conversation.
These are not *steps* to hearing God, but ways of directing our
focus and attention so that we can stay connected to God and
receive what he has for us. These four things are:

Focusing: Quieting our soul and focusing the eyes of our heart
on God.

Listening: Paying attention to the promptings of the Spirit while
actively reflecting on spiritual matters.

Discerning: Taking notice of both the process and the content
of our conversation.

Responding: Doing something with what we are receiving.

Focusing is turning our heart and mind toward God as we
intentionally engage with him. We give him our full attention, just
as we would anyone with whom we intend to have a serious

conversation. Our purposeful focus is necessary in order for us to grasp the full significance of what he wants to say to us.

Quieting and focusing are important aspects of listening, because God seldom tries to compete with the noise in our mind or overpower our thoughts. The deliberate decision to focus is part of how we seek him out from among the many things that vie for our attention. The injunction to "seek me with your whole heart" (Jer.29:13) really applies here. God is *God*. It only makes sense that we would need to stop what we are doing once in a while and focus all of our heart and mind on him.

Listening is the actual process of interacting with God and hearing what he wants to say to us. This is by no means a passive act. As we will see, listening is a two-way conversation much like we would expect to have with a wise mentor. Our part in this process is important, because if we simply empty our mind and wait for something to strike us, we will probably be *too disengaged* to receive anything. On the other hand, if we try too hard to guess or figure out what God might say, we may be *too preoccupied* to see or hear what God is showing us. Effective listening requires active reflection, a lot of curiosity, a willingness to be transparent, and seasoned discernment.

Discerning is not about preventing things from going wrong or keeping our conversation "safe." Rather, it is more about noticing what is going on in our conversation and making decisions about what to do with our observations.

Within the limits of our human abilities, we do not have the power to prevent wrong thoughts or mistaken ideas from entering our mind. Our job is not to "get it right" so that God will not be disappointed in us. Instead, we need to trust that God is able to call our attention to the quality of our thoughts throughout a conversation and show us what is true and right. It is alright to learn the way Peter did, by blurting out what is on our mind and then learning from the Master where we are on target and where we are missing the mark. Discerning is mostly about paying attention and remaining teachable so that anything we come up with can either be confirmed or revised.

Responding in some way to our time together helps anchor the conversation in our soul and increases its impact on our life. This can be as simple as a prayer of thanksgiving or as extensive as making restitution for something we have done. Often, writing out a prayer or making a note to remind us of what we have received will go a long way toward helping us connect our insights with the real world. We can even ask God to help us discover other life-giving ways to respond to what he has given us.

As we learn how to incorporate each of these four areas into our prayer life, our conversations with God will develop and mature. And as we engage with him, he will reveal himself to us, heal the broken places in our heart, fill the empty spaces in our soul, and bring us to a place of joy and peace that we have never before experienced. All of this will happen within the context of a vibrant relationship that has the potential to grow throughout our lifetime.

Now that you have the big picture, in the next chapter we will listen in on a few more conversations with God so that you get more of the flavor of these interactions. After that, we will re-visit each of these four aspects of conversational prayer in more detail. My hope is that by then you will have what you need in order to begin (or renew) your own conversations with God. If at any time you want to dig deeper or want some additional help in these areas, you can pick and choose from the remaining chapters as needed or desired.

I hope I can convey to you how important – how utterly essential – I believe this form of prayer is for each one of us. This is not just some spiritual exercise that would make for an interesting afternoon, or a spiritual gift reserved only for super Christians. *This is your birthright as a child of God – to feed your soul and bring you closer to God.*

God speaks today because we need him, personally, in ways that are tangible and substantive. His presence with us is much more than an idea or a theological premise. It is an actual living reality that we can truly experience, and from which we will receive food and water for our soul if we learn how to engage with him.[1] God wants so much to have an authentic relationship with us that he moved heaven and earth to bridge the gulf between him and us. And a big part of what he wants in that relationship is to talk with us and speak into our lives. I pray that this will be the start of a much deeper relationship with him than you have ever known.

God, I ask You right now to open up my spirit to Your presence, to Your heart for me, Your word for me. Help my unbelief. Calm my fear. Help me to see how incredibly safe I am in Your grace for me. Fan the flames of my desire, so that I want You even more. I want so much to hear Your voice and to know Your heart. Impress this hope deep into my soul. Open my eyes and ears to receive whatever You have for me. In Jesus' name ...

---

[1] "Listen to me and eat what is good ... delight yourself in the richest of fare" (Isa.55).

PERSONAL REFLECTION

If you could have conversations with God and ask him about your past and present struggles, what would you want to talk about? What would you want him to help you with?

DISCUSSION QUESTIONS

What is your impression of people who say, "God told me something"?

What negative experiences have you had personally (or seen in others) in regard to "hearing" God?

What positive experiences have you had (or seen) in regard to hearing God's voice?

What reservations do you have about conversational prayer?

EXERCISE

Read Isaiah 55. This chapter says a lot about what God's voice can do. Identify as many things as you can. Many of those things are presented as metaphors. How do you suppose they might flesh out in real life?

List all of the imperatives (commands) that you see in Isaiah 55. Taken together, what do you see in them?

Reading between the lines, what does Isaiah 55 reveal to us about God's heart?

Chapter 2 – Listening in on Real Conversations

"Let me hear Your loving kindness in the morning; For I trust in You; Teach me the way in which I should walk; For to You I lift up my soul" (Ps.143:8 NASB).

What you are about to read in the following pages are actual entries from personal journals, my own as well as others. They are presented here with the hope that in reading them you will see how amazingly normal they are as well as how beautifully uplifting and life-giving they were when these conversations took place in real time.

I am also hopeful that by walking through these examples, you will discover (or rediscover) a way of conversing with God that is truly accessible to you – that as you read you may find yourself saying, "This is something I can do!"

To help you get the most out of these entries, I would like to preface them with a few comments. First, although they did require a little editing to make them more readable (journals can be really messy!) each one has been preserved as much as possible in its original form in order to better convey the kind of process that might go on while having a conversation with God. As such, you will see a lot of inconsistencies in punctuation, capitalization, and grammar, as well as incomplete sentences.

Second, because there are often a lot of things going on in a person's mind that never make it to their journal, some annotations have been inserted to help you see more of the process, such as when the writer felt a need to change directions or when they felt resistance, and so on. These annotations have been phrased as if they could have been part of the original text, but they are enclosed within brackets [like this] so you will have no difficulty telling the original journal entry from the annotations.

Finally, I would ask you to read through these reflections slowly and carefully so that you can enter into the original experience as much as possible. I would even suggest pausing after each one to reflect on it for a few moments before going on the the next one.

It would be easy to miss the significance of any one of these, because the conversations were very specific to the spiritual state of the person at the time they were interacting with God. The less you share of their particular frame of reference, the more difficult it will be for you to see the ways in which their conversation was important to them. By reading these reflections slowly and thoughtfully, you may be able to better appreciate what they were experiencing.

My prayer for you is that as you read these reflections, they will be as life-giving for you as they were for the person who initially wrote them down.

Commitment and Reluctance

[Setting: This entry resulted from trying to have a conversation with God on a day when the writer did not feel like doing it. Rather than force his way through his time, he chose instead to talk to God about his reluctance.]

As I sit down to have my quiet time, I feel a lot of internal resistance to doing this today. Wondering why I am having so much trouble. Been reading Isaiah one and I can hear God's cry over the unfaithfulness of Israel. The word *uncommitted* rings true for me as well. I am pained at the sound of the word, though.

Why am I so uncommitted after so many years of seeking God? This is so important! What are the roots of my reluctance? Holy Spirit, come and reveal my heart.

[Suddenly the whole issue seems to turn upside down. It almost takes my breath away.]

Oh .... where has there *not* been reluctance. Almost every serious commitment I made in the first 35 years of my life was costly and regrettable. And whatever commitments I have made that were good have mostly been lost. Only in recent years have I seen commitments that offered any hope. Of course I'm reluctant!

They seem like lose-lose propositions to me, because either (1) the other person betrays my commitment; or (2) I suffer some eventual loss due to what it costs to stay connected. But having no commitment means no meaningful relationship. So I can't win.

[My eye scans my earlier notes and I remember that I began this conversation thinking about my reluctance regarding God, not people.]

God cannot fail me or leave me or drain me. And clearly I do not know this in my soul (otherwise I would not feel such reluctance).

[A verse comes to mind.]

"If you only knew who it was who speaks to you" (Jn.4:10).

[I stop to pray a prayer of confession about how poorly I must know him.]

[I feel led to make a list of people with whom I have had commitments that were painful. With each one I say out loud, "God, you are not like that person."]

[Now I feel led to write a short psalm to God.]

You are the faithful one – compassionate Father, unmovable in purpose, and committed to me. Committed to being my Lord the way I most need. Committed to breathing Life into my body. You truly love me. The way I always needed to be loved. I want to let you in. I open myself to receive You.

[I'm feeling closer to God now. Reflecting back on the last few minutes, I see how different my time was than what I expected it would be.]

I have to smile now, because I so loved our time together today and I was so reluctant when we started. There is not enough time to spend with You.

I just realized what an affront it is to *not* commit to You. Forgive my foolish heart, O God. Remold/Remake my heart to be wholly Yours. I want Your sweet presence in my mind and heart. Thank You for Your gifts to me.

A New Look at Rest

[Setting: This is an example of how being completely honest about our reactions to a passage of Scripture can lead to some unexpected insights.]

"He makes me lie down in green pastures" (Ps.23)

Lie down? How can I be of any good lying down?
I need to be up doing something. I need to be involved. There's so much to do. Why are we lying down?
He makes me lie down. This is *Your* idea. But why? Why would You think lying down is such a good idea?
Yes, I understand the need to rest. But that doesn't fit right now. What do you want me to see here?
I go back to my initial question. Isn't there lots to do?

Lord, I can't seem to reconcile these opposing feelings – the need to rest and the need to work.

[A new thought jumps into my mind – that rest and work are not necessarily mutually exclusive.]

There's work *in us* that God wants to do that needs *rest* in order to do its work.

[That hits me like a new insight.]

[Now it feels like I'm being taught.]

God gives green grass and still water – in abundance – for my soul – not just to energize me to do stuff – but so the good things He has fed me can do its work *in me*. I need to remember I'm part of His target mission, too – I'm a recipient, too. Not just a minister or messenger of the mission. I'm not just resting in order to recharge. I'm resting so He can work in me in ways that do not happen when I'm busy.

[I feel led to respond.]

So Lord, help me to lie down and be still – to let Your Word and Your Life do its work in me. Let me receive. To digest. To give this some time so that what You gave me can percolate through all the cells of my body and every part of my soul. To let You deep into my heart – in peace – in secure receptivity of Your heart for me in this Holy Place, pure and set apart to Be With You.

Reflecting on God's Goodness in My Life

[Setting: Here is an example of how identifying personally with the text can help us internalize our real identity in Christ.]

"For as the earth brings forth its shoots, and as a garden causes what is sown in it to spring up, so the Lord God will cause

righteousness and praise to spring up before all the nations."
(Isa.61:11)

[What comes to mind is a way of identifying with the passage.]

I too am a garden of God. He has sown good things into my
heart and they are beginning to break through the top soil and
reach and grow up toward the Light.

And what was it He sowed? [Asking simple questions often
open new doors to insights.] "Good news, binding up, liberty,
release, favor, comfort, garland, oil of gladness, mantle of praise,
rebuilding, repairing" [These phrases came from looking back at
verses near the beginning of the chapter.]

What an amazing God! He not only rescued me from the
death-like bondage that I experienced in my youth, but he planted
within me things that could grow and become a source of Life. So
I could become what was always intended for me, to be a pleasant
place for God to dwell and show His love to the world.

[Again looking back at various phrases from 61:1-4.]
No longer "oppressed ... broken-hearted ... captive ... prisoner ...
in mourning ... in ashes ... ruined ... devastated."

These memories are still fresh, and my heart still wavers and
holds delusions of life because of them, [confessing what is true
without any condemnation] *but the vines, the little saplings – they
are growing!*
*I see Life! I see Hope! I see Purpose and Wonder. This is my
Redeemer's Life and Work in me. And there is no other way I would
rather live.*
[Here I just rested for a while, enjoying the feeling of hope and
rejoicing in what God had done for me.]

What it Might Have Looked Like on the Outskirts of Bethlehem a Very Long Time Ago

[Setting: This journal entry came from the desire to enter into the Christmas story and experience more of the drama of that event. While to some it might look more like creative fiction than a reflection, its value comes from the writer's ability to experience some of the wonder of God coming to earth as an infant (a story that loses its charm for many of us after hearing it so many times). Also important is the fact that the writer had no idea where the story was going when he began. It came to him as he imagined being in this place and time.]

"Hush, my friend. Be very quiet – listen with all your heart. It would be so easy to miss what's happening here. You would never know from just a glance – you might dismiss it as far too poor a scene to hold such great promise for all of us.

"Shush! Careful! Can you see? Do you see it? Over there, in the stall, in the soft light of the lamp. You wouldn't think it mattered – but an hour ago there were shepherds all over that place. And boy, were they excited! They were falling over themselves with glee.

"Now it's quiet again. The mom and dad can't seem to get enough of looking at their new baby, though clearly they have had a very long day. The way she keeps pulling him close, as if she can scarcely believe he is real. And the silent tears – so much has gone on here – and there is so much more to be known.

"But you and I, my friend, we need to stay here and let them have this moment of peace. It is far too sacred to disturb them one more time – though I don't know exactly why. So we will just watch this beautiful sight from our vantage point, and wonder what mystery might lie within it.

"But do not miss it, my friend. Mark this night and remember it well. For one thing I am sure of – nothing will ever be the same. And this place, right here, has something to do with why that is.

"Shh! Listen!"

[Right now my heart is alive to so much more of the mystery and wonder of God's intervention. I think I'll just sit here a while and let it soak in.]

Psalm 23: Overflowing Cup – Celebration with Extravagance

[Setting: The following is an example of how we can take a familiar passage and paraphrase it in our own words so that it becomes more meaningful and accessible to our heart. In this case, we see a rhythm emerge in which the writer takes each phrase of the psalm, reflects on it and amplifies it, and connects with each element of the psalm as personally as possible.]

Psalm 23.
The Lord is my Shepherd, I shall not want
You make me lie down in green pastures
You lead me beside still waters
Your rod and your staff – they comfort me
You restore my soul
Surely goodness and mercy will follow me all the days of my life

Oh Lord, You are my Shepherd. [I stop and hold that thought, anticipating that God will unpack it and reveal himself more.] That means I am indeed a sheep and therefore in need of a shepherd along with the rest of the flock. There is to me the

Shepherd of me.[2] I will not be left behind, abandoned, will not be alone or defenseless. I will be provided for by *His* provision. . . You bring me to the green pastures and say "This is where we rest" – where you lie down – where you graze and are safe/secure enough to actually lie down and take a load off.

You lead me beside still waters – serenity and even a mirror for our journey where I can see the reflection of You in the lead and me following behind You. Still waters make for quite a refreshing drink as well as a calming back drop setting. The waves are not churning. Shalom ... [Once again there is a settling, and then I sense that it's time to move forward.]

You restore my soul. The world depletes me deep inside and yet there is a restoration of the deepest part of my soul when I'm found in Your love. *You* restore – too big a job for me – too impossible. In any language.

You lead me in the paths of righteousness for the sake of Your name. It's actually Your righteousness – of You, for You, with You – in me! Even though I walk through the darkest valley I will fear no evil. I will not be afraid. No evil – big or small is to be feared and rob me of Love Bonds. Why? You are with me, in me, for me, near me, indwelling me. You are being Immanuel. The One to whom I matter greatly. You are Crea*tor* – the rest is merely crea*ted*, including the baaaa sheep – me.

Your rod and Your staff – they comfort me. Rod keeps me on the path of the journey – *Your* rod (again a God-sized job not at all sized for me) and *Your* staff (used to bring the sheep back when they do wander from Your flock). I get to belong and rejoin the group *no matter what!*

You prepare a table before me in the face of my enemies. The ones who hate and dislike me watch as You set the table and

---

[2] This unusual wording is from a rich Hebrew idiom where instead of "my shepherd" one would say, "there is to me (or for me) a shepherd."

prepare the fare which will be consumed. You anoint my head with oil. Blessing and anointing – isn't that usually for the "special guest"? This is the Prodigal Son's banquet/party and it's part of the restoration of my whole self. Reconciled back to *You* as well as to the flock. My cup runneth over – abundance is not equal to scarcity. Again Love replaces fear. Perfect Love – Yours, casts out the fear.

Surely – most assuredly with more assurances than Carter has pills [an idiom based on an old product, meaning "a lot."] – goodness and mercy will follow me all the days of my life. All my born days – there will be goodness (from You of course) and Your mercy – (not judgment and punishment). Every day – today, yesterday, tomorrow, and day after that and day after day after day – the dailiness is the most seductive of all. And I will dwell, inhabit, be found in Your house = *Ha Beit Shel Adonai*[3] Himself. The one You built – where You are to be found ... where You are being found. The home address for me is the very same address You have – this is a forever promise, an ever and ever and evermore proposition and relationship of the deepest order.

[Coming to the end of the Psalm, I feel refreshed with his Living Water.]

What Jesus Kept When He Came to Earth

[Setting: In the following example, the writer was reflecting on the well-known passage from Philippians where Paul described how Jesus came to earth. Each sentence seemed to flow from the prior one, with no idea where it would lead.]

---

[3] Hebrew for "The House of the Lord."

"He was in the form of God ... yet he emptied himself"
(Phil.2:1-11).

What an incomprehensible move on the part of God.

His position in the universe goes beyond "having rights."

He was Owner, Creator, and Ruler of All.

Yet he subjected himself to the life of one who owned nothing, who ultimately gave up his voice in regard to his own body ... to experience the worst that this world and our enemy could do.

To let us know in no uncertain terms that the enemy does not have the last word! That life is more than self-protection and self-importance.

That there is LIFE the enemy Cannot Destroy!

Life that is not just "possible" but a present / historical reality.

He emptied himself. What an easily missed phrase. This is the equivalent of stripping a nebula down to a small rock.

And I am afraid of having my peace disturbed by an unwelcome phone call or necessary errand; or having my dignity bruised by a misunderstanding; or my need not met in the moment I feel it. I am afraid to give; I guard my space; I hoard my resources.

Lord, free me from my foolish beliefs and attachments to such things as what I possess or what I fear.

As I think about what You had left – You pared down to just one thing – *nothing was left but Your relationship with Your Father!* There was nothing else. You had nothing else. *And it was enough!*

To sustain You, yes. But to give You more than enough to give away LIFE as it has never been given before or since; to give You more than enough to face death on a cross and live through it – right up to the point of death.

Your relationship to Your Father was enough to change the world! You had the only thing You needed – the only thing that

mattered. To make sure we did not confuse Life with anything else
– (but we still do!).
What LIFE! What glory! What hope!
YES! YES! YES! YES!
I want that, too! I want that, too!

Receive me, O Lord, into Your hands – into Your care – into
Your heart. Let me live as if the only thing that matters is my
connection to YOU.

Looking to Jesus

[Setting: This is a rather lengthy entry that I wrote out during a
one-day retreat with a small group. Its real value here is in showing
how spending more than a few minutes can be very valuable. Most
of the good stuff came only after turning things over in my mind
and asking a lot of questions. In the process, I learned a lot about
the nature of true joy.]

"Since we are surrounded by so great a cloud of witnesses ...
Looking to Jesus the pioneer and perfecter of our faith, who for
the joy that was set before him endured the cross ... and has taken
his seat at the right hand of the throne of God" (Heb. 12:1-3).

[I began by thinking about the context of these verses, especially
that they follow the famous "Hall of Faith" chapter where a lot of
old saints are listed along with how they endured great hardship as
they looked forward to that which Jesus would bring.]
This "great cloud of witnesses" all endured suffering. So the image
of "looking to Jesus" is not about seeing him in his glorified state,

it is asking us to consider how Jesus *endured* such suffering. The author is trying to encourage his readers and listeners to endure hardship well.

"Enduring" means making it through to the end. "Fixing our eyes on Jesus" is not just in reference to the event of the cross, but it does encompass the event of the cross.

[So far I am making observations about various words and phrases, trying to dig deeper into the meaning of the text. I have a sense that there is something very important here that I have not yet grasped.]

Jesus, who endured *horrific* suffering, the absolute worst torture the ancients had found. He who had no sin, no fault, no cause for so much hatred to be directed at him.

[Trying to grasp some sense of meaning for what he "endured."]
[Some questions begin to come to mind.]

How? By what means did he *endure* such unimaginable torment?
For the Joy? What joy? What did you see?
What did you fix *Your* eyes on?

[Some possible answers start coming to mind.]

– the realities of heaven
– seeing Your Father
– the future
– the redemption of all [this hits me with the force of an insight]

"If my death will bring about the salvation of many, then count me in!" [I imagine him in the garden of Gethsemane coming to this kind of conclusion.]

This is the standard for what it means to endure. No, that doesn't sound right. [I noticed that the words did not capture my impression, so I tried again.] More like – Nothing He asks of me is beyond reason, or remotely close to what He Himself endured.

[Another thought comes to mind about endurance.]

Enduring occurs in two dimensions – *duration* and *intensity*.
1. to persist through something and come out the other side
(duration). 2. to hold up under the weight of something (intensity).
[More questions again.]
Joy: What joy? From Where? How did You find it?
"For the joy set before Him" of redeeming the earth!
[Suddenly I get a glimpse of this through my own experience.]
I have tasted of this kind of joy when people say my book [*The
Truth About Lies and Lies About Truth*] has touched them, set
them free, or captivated their heart. It feels so good to give life to
others. To see them heal and recover. It warms my heart.
Oh, the JOY of destroying the Destroyer – of pushing back the
Darkness – of witnessing the Dawning Light.
The joy Jesus must have felt, crushing death beneath His feet.
HE WON!
By enduring, overcoming, trusting in his Father, right up to His
departure – His death.
He won! He cheated death. No, He destroyed death, the power of
death. Death and hell and suffering could not break Him.
What's more, He nailed sin to the cross.

[What comes to mind here is a new idea that there are two things
going on simultaneously at the cross – His agonizing death in the
physical realm, and the defeat of the enemy in the spiritual realm.]
"Set your sights on the realities of heaven" (Col.3:1 NLT)
[That phrase jumps to mind because it tells me to look beyond
the physical world to understand reality.]
While in the earthly realm His body was being tormented, in the
heavenly, unseen realm, He was crushing the serpent's head!

This isn't about enduring suffering for the sake of becoming an
"endurer" or to prove you can do it. It is dying to self in the act of

destroying evil. *Doing whatever it takes* to destroy the enemy, to break the power of evil in people's lives so that they can be free – so they can live in Light instead of Darkness.

Even just the anticipation of redemption was enough to inspire the Old Testament saints to endure; the faith/belief/trust that God would vindicate Himself and all that is good.

This is the incentive to do good – to do for others – to be part of healing, serving, feeding, drilling wells around the world, etc.

To be willing to be uncomfortable or to suffer so that Good may come.

[My preferred definition of *Love* is, "the will for the good of another" – so I extended this to create a definition for *Joy*.]

JOY is love realized, love enabled, the good of another made real or fulfilled. JOY is seeing that will for the good of another come to fruition. This is why love for another brings joy.

We rejoice in Goodness being manifest in the world, and the privilege of being instrumental in that Good coming about.

[I think of an email I received recently that contained a heart-warming story where people unexpectedly came around a down-syndrome boy and gave him a real experience of love just a few months before he died. It made me rejoice to think of such goodness being given. That's why I think JOY is the fulfillment of Love.]

YES. I want to be your instrument, to bring life to those who are dead and light to those in darkness.

YES, Lord.

Jesus saw what He was going to do for the world. And for that JOY He endured the cross.

Because He knew it was worth it!

That is why we can be OK with suffering when we do well. It's worth it.

Doing good can be inconvenient or costly. But it's worth it.

For the joy of bringing Good things into the world.

[At this point I feel very full, very soul-fed.]

This all makes sense of the verses that say "rejoice when you suffer for doing well." This is incentive that spurs me on to do well, even when it feels like too much to do. This is a lot more powerful than "I *should*" do something. I endure because I *want* to see something good and joyful come to fruition.

[I am noticing how what started out as a reflection and an attempt to grasp the meaning of "endure" ended up being a teaching about the nature of JOY and an understanding of suffering for well-doing that I had not had before.]

Thank you God for those amazing insights into Your heart for us. Thank you for the life that You brought into those moments I just read about. Thank You for what You will do in me. Give me ears to hear and eyes to see so that I too can receive what You have for me. In Jesus' name....

PERSONAL REFLECTION

What reactions do you have toward the reflections in this chapter?

DISCUSSION QUESTIONS

How do you suppose the writers were impacted by the insights that arose from their engagement with God?

How do these reflections differ from what you have thought about in the past regarding hearing from God?

Have you ever used a journal as part of your spiritual journey?
If so, what was your experience? How are these entries similar to or different from your own?
If not, would you consider using one if it helped you focus your conversations with God?

EXERCISE

Write a letter to God, telling Him the deepest longings of your heart as you contemplate the hope of hearing from Him.

Talk about your desire to be led by the Spirit, your desire to know Him better, and your desire to feel His presence with you.

If you have any sense of his response to you, feel free to write that out as well.

Chapter 3 – Four Aspects
of Conversations With God

"Incline your ear and come to Me. Listen, that you may live"
(Isa.55:3).

Conversational prayer has an elegance and simplicity to it that
many people begin to experience with relatively little difficulty
once they have been pointed in the right direction. In fact many
are pleasantly surprised at how readily accessible God really is to
them – they just need a little encouragement and a few guidelines
to get started.

With that in mind, these next few pages are intended to
provide you with just the help you may have needed in order to
begin your journey into the sort of working relationship with God
that your true heart has always longed for. God never meant for
this to be as rare or difficult to engage in as many of us have been
led to believe. Once we get past the simplicity of talking with God
and embrace his way of relating to us, a little encouragement and
instruction can go a long way.

In Chapter One, I gave you a very brief introduction to the
four aspects of conversations with God. My goal in this chapter is
to describe these areas with enough depth and detail so that you
will be able to engage in serious conversations with God by the
time you are finished reading it. I also hope you will try the
exercise at the end of this chapter, as this will help you walk
through the process and identify any specific areas you may want
to know more about.

Focusing: Quieting our soul and focusing the eyes of our heart
on God.

Listening: Paying attention to the promptings of the Spirit while
actively reflecting on spiritual matters.

Discerning: Taking notice of both the process and the content
of our conversation.

Responding: Doing something with what we are receiving.

FOCUSING

Focusing is about turning our heart and mind toward God as we
intentionally engage with him. We believe that he is truly with us
in the moment and anticipate that our soul will be fed with food
and water from his voice and his presence. We trust his good
heart, trust that he is *for* us, and trust that he holds us in love and
desires to be with us. We believe that his plan to redeem all that
was lost includes *us* and the broken places in our life. His main
reason for redeeming us was to have a meaningful relationship
with us. That is why we can count on him to meet us when we
turn our heart toward him.

For most people, to focus well means that we must also quiet
our mind and let go of the many thoughts that would otherwise
demand our attention. In doing so, we make a space for engaging
with God that is holy and receptive. Fortunately, quieting and
focusing have a kind of synergistic affect, such that one helps to
improve our ability to do the other. As we calm our thoughts we
are generally able to focus better, and as we begin to envision his
presence with us, we tend to become more peaceful and let go of
the distractions in our mind.

Learning how to quiet our mind and focus on God and the
things of God is an essential part of engaging in fruitful

conversation with him. But most of us have never been shown how to do this, so we may feel at a loss as to how to begin. In addition, many people harbor perceptions of God that are too abstract or harsh to override any fear or distrust they have, so focusing on God can be something of a challenge.

At any given moment we may have a lot more stuff buzzing around in our head than we wish. Some of it may be due to the work we do for a living, some of it comes at us from our media-blitz culture, and some is the result of our own efforts to multitask or to distract ourselves from the pressures we feel.

Since most of the time God speaks to us in a "still, small voice," any buildup of mental "static" in our head from anxiety, stress or other factors can really get in the way of hearing him. That is why it is so important to quiet our mind and deliberately turn our attention toward God. We need to tune out the outside demands, let go of our "to-do" lists, slow down our pace, and calm our mind and body. At the same time we need to begin turning our thoughts toward God with the confidence that he is very much with us and wants to talk to us.

A great analogy for Focusing can be seen in the field of electronics where this process is often referred to as *improving the signal-to-noise ratio*. We need to lower the "noise" level and increase the "signal" level so that we can hear what God is "sending" us. It reminds me of trying to tune into an AM radio station that has a lot of surrounding static (although not many people listen to AM radio anymore).

For the most part, learning how to quiet ourselves is a natural capability we have as human beings. With a little practice, most of us can put aside the things that are running through our head and deliberately calm our mind and body for a few minutes. Often it helps to take a few deep breaths, close our eyes, or relax our shoulders as we clear our mind of any pressing thoughts.

Not everyone finds this to be an easy task, however. I once heard someone say that whenever he tries to quiet his mind, he finds this highly-caffeinated chihuahua running around in his head, yapping incessantly. If you can identify with his difficulty, this may take more effort or even some outside help before you can do this well. But it is a skill worth learning, not only for the sake of conversational prayer, but for your own peace of mind.

Just to be clear, not everyone needs to become perfectly quiet in order to hear God's voice. There are some people who have a high-energy personality by nature, and are able to pay attention very well on multiple levels at the same time. They may even find that attempting to quiet feels like shutting down altogether, or that it is more distracting than helpful. If this describes you at all, then please do not take on the burden of trying to force yourself to do something that is counterproductive. After all, the point is to have enough presence of mind to be able to notice the promptings of the Spirit, not to see how much you can quiet your nervous system.

Improving Our Focus

In addition to clearing our mind of whatever "noise" is there, we need to turn our heart and our thoughts toward God and focus on him.[4] In order to do that effectively, we must first recognize that God is right here with us and in us. Even though most Christians agree in principle that God is everywhere, in practice many respond to him as if he is far away and hard to reach. When they pray, they feel like they are talking to an empty room or to someone who is up in outer space somewhere. But the truth is that God is already here even before we pray. He is in us and around us, inhabiting every cell of our body.

---

[4] "Fixing our eyes on Jesus" (Heb.12:2).

Our heart stance here is really important. This is not a long-distance conversation, but one we are having by faith with someone who is with us right here in the room and in our very being. "Those who come to God must believe that he is present with them, and that he willingly responds to those who want to engage with him" (Heb.11:6 paraphrase).

If we believe God is far off in space somewhere, chances are we will have a hard time sensing his heart for us or believing we can hear him. Or, if we have doubts about whether God wants to be anywhere near us, we will have great difficulty believing that he has anything to give us. On the other hand, if we believe God is right here, that he engulfs us with his presence and wants to connect with us in love, then our heart and mind will be far more expectant and receptive to whatever he has for us.

Those who have a good image of God as a loving Father can usually do this more easily. We can lean back and relax in him the way an anxious child might lean into a trustworthy parent and be calmed by their embrace. In doing so, we can experience peace like that which comes from being with someone who loves us fully and in whom we totally trust.

If your image of God is not so secure, let me suggest another way of approaching him. Try to think of God as someone who you do not know very well yet, but that you would like to get to know because you have heard such good things about him. While you still may not be entirely sure about this, you have decided to try to find out for yourself. That way you can be as cautious as you need to be and still get close enough to get to know him and have conversations with him. I think you will find that he is actually very receptive to timid hearts.

Thankfully, focusing is not limited to our ability to direct our thoughts. We can also ask God to *help* us open up our heart and mind to him. Each of us has a built-in protection system that works below the conscious level of our mind to keep people and things that seem too big for us or beyond our control at a distance. For many people, God falls into that category. We may even believe we have a lot of good reasons for keeping him at arm's length, however impossible that may be. Asking him to calm our fears and help us let down our guard is an important part of giving him full access to our heart and putting ourselves in a willing place of receiving.

We can tell him that what we really want is to experience his presence with us, just as if we were sitting on the mountain with his disciples, listening to him teach. Or perhaps you might envision the two of you alone together as you pour out your heart about something only he can hear. Maybe you need comfort and want him to hold you or perhaps sit next to you so you can lean into him and feel his strength sustaining you.

These are all legitimate ways of being with God. He is already fully present, so picturing him near you and surrounding you in every way is really just a willingness to see the unseen.[5] Asking him to meet us in this way can even be thought of as a prayer request in the form of a picture. Or we can ask him for a video of us together that *he* wants us to have, so that we can go beyond *our* wishes for the relationship and instead receive more of his desire for us. Either way, there is no reason why we should not ask for what we want.

Another way to improve our focus is to bring to mind an experience we have had that brings with it feelings of gratitude or appreciation. As we connect with and re-experience those emotions, we align our heart and mind with the goodness of God in our life. We can then approach God more fully engaged and more open to receive from him.

---

[5] The psalmist once envisioned God this way, "You hem me in behind and before" (Ps.139:5).

Quieting and focusing are important elements of hearing well. We need to be fairly deliberate about making this space to connect with God, otherwise our time with him will seem more like a task to accomplish than a relational experience. And most people will need to stop and refocus from time to time throughout their conversation with God in order to maintain their connection. Once we learn how to do this and get a taste of what it is like to simply be with God, we will find that focusing becomes something we truly enjoy on its own.

LISTENING

We now come to the very heart of the matter. *How* does God speak to us? What does his voice sound like? How do we listen? What are we listening for? How does this all work?

This is where things really get exciting! If you have ever felt him touch your heart, you know how much life and joy can come from direct contact with God. When he speaks into our life, we are changed in ways that we could never bring about on our own. And the good news is that we can open a space for this to happen more often than we ever thought possible.

Let me begin by saying two things that will set the context for this section. First, *listening to the Spirit of God is a way of interacting with him that develops with experience.* An appropriate analogy might be learning to play the violin. Proper pressure on the bow and precise placement of the fingers on the strings can be very hard to do at first, but over time it gradually becomes second nature to the student. Similarly, the more we converse with God, the more sensitive we will become to the movements of the Spirit and the nuances of God's voice. So our best strategy for learning how to hear God's voice is to meet with him as often as we can.

Second, trying to explain a spiritual experience on paper is somewhat challenging. Please keep in mind that I am trying to do more than simply convey information about prayer. My hope is that you will get a sense for what this can be like and try working through the exercises and experience God for yourself.

How Does God Speak to Us?

The short answer to this question is this: *The way God communicates with us most often is Spirit-to-spirit.* His Spirit engages directly with our spirit and reveals to us what we need for life. As pointed out earlier, Spirit-to-spirit communication is both similar and dissimilar to person-to-person communication. Let's begin with a couple of references to this kind of connection found in the New Testament.

> "The *Spirit himself testifies with our spirit* that we are the children of God" (Rom.8:16, emphasis added).

> "This is what we speak, not in words taught us by human wisdom but in words *taught by the Spirit, expressing spiritual truths in spiritual words ... discerned spiritually"* (1Cor.2:13-14, paraphrase and emphasis added).

Notice that these verses are *not* talking about preaching and teaching or any other form of human communication, or even about reading the Bible. This is about direct interaction between the Spirit of God and our spirit. Personally, I wish Paul had gone on to describe just *how* God "testifies with our spirit" and what those "spiritual words" are like or how they are "discerned." I suspect the main reason he did not do that was because most of his original readers and listeners already knew what he meant; they had been mentored in this kind of prayer before.

What we *do* have that sheds light on these verses is the testimony of literally thousands of people over the centuries whose lives have been transformed by learning how to listen to the Spirit of God. Some of the most well-known names in Christian history have known the power of God directly in their lives and been changed by his revelations to them (Edman). Almost universally they confess that they experienced God's revelations to them primarily in the form of spontaneous impressions, words, and images in their mind. When we look at the fruit of their lives, we can see that God was definitely at work in them. So we can with great confidence identify this as Spirit-to-spirit communication.

An important thing to notice here is that sensing God's voice is not a sensational kind of event. It does not require a special spiritual gift of prophecy or laying on of hands. Nor is it something that takes control of your mind or vocal chords. Most Christians who hear from God both regularly and reliably, report that his words are usually received in a fairly peaceful but spontaneous manner. We know these thoughts and images are from God because of the way they feed our soul and cause life to spring forth, like water on a dry plant. His words have a ring of truth to them and a quality that is beyond what we would normally come up with on our own. Often the very words and concepts seem unusual and beyond our normal way of thinking.

Sometimes his word begins as an impression that arises in us with a sense of hope and then gracefully unfolds into words like a spring of water rushing up out of the ground. The awareness of what God wants us to know may dawn on our conscious mind rather gradually like a sunrise, and only later do we find words to describe what we have received. Other times, we experience a stunning clarity in the words themselves, as if they had been spoken by another person in the room. Quite often an image, an icon or even a short mental video will jump into our mind that embodies what God wants to reveal to us. He may also remind us of a song, connect our present thoughts to a memory, or speak to us in any number of other ways.

What all of these various ways of receiving from God have in common is that God's voice is generally *experienced* as much as it is *heard*. We may feel surprised by the unexpected thought, or get the sense that someone turned on a light – an "Aha!" experience that tells us this is really different.

Returning to our earlier comment that none of this is sensational or extraordinary, conversational prayer is actually a relatively small step beyond pondering or reflecting on a portion of God's Word. If we know how to turn something over and over in our mind while being curious about what we are observing and willing to be impacted by what we discover, then we may already have most of what we need in order to learn how to hear his voice. As you will see, this kind of spiritual reflection forms a very substantial context from which we can begin to have real conversations with God.

Using Scripture to Begin Our Conversations

One of the best ways to tune in to God and hear his voice is to learn how to engage in careful spiritual reflection. As we focus on a verse of Scripture or some issue for which we need discernment, we turn it over in our mind and reflect on it in various ways with the expectation that God will join us and engage in that experience with us. Somewhere in the process we begin to take notice of things we had not seen before, or we may receive an insight or a thought that clears up some confusion we have had.

These thoughts are often accompanied by feelings of gratitude or joy, or even a profound sense of peace. When the insight proves to be life-giving and fruitful, we know that we have heard from God. Over time, we learn to identify the nature of those insights and the force that is inherent within them, which then in subsequent conversations allows us to more readily discern when our thoughts are from God rather than from our own creative mind.

For example, Chapter Two included a reflection from Philippians where we have the famous description of Jesus leaving heaven and coming to earth as a servant. As I reflected on that passage, I began by trying to focus on what Jesus might have gone through in order to become human. Did he lay aside certain godly attributes, like the ability to be in more than one place at a time? What exactly does it mean that he "emptied himself"?

Reaching for a better question, what came to mind was, "What did he *have left* when he was done emptying himself?" He left a heavenly realm where he never felt hunger or pain or scarcity of any good thing, and lived as a wanderer without a home or possessions of any kind except the clothes he wore. Did he keep anything at all?

Then the thought hit me, "He still had his relationship with his Father!" In fact, that is just about all Jesus had left of his prior state. *Yet that was enough to change the world!* It struck me with all the force of a huge wave. Wow!

Clearly, this had the tone and character of God in both the process I was engaged in as well as the life-giving thought that came out of it. The insight had a way of hammering home *how incredibly important our relationship with God is*. At the same time, I could not say that I actually "heard" anything. This was a spontaneous thought about the nature and significance of Jesus' incarnation that I had never seen before – an insight that could only have come from God.

Since all of Scripture originated with God and has the potential to unleash his life in us, it is the perfect place to begin our conversations with him. And who can better reveal to us the treasures there than the Spirit of God himself?

How Do I Get Started?

There are several good examples in Scripture that illustrate how we can engage in conversation with God. Many of the Psalms are beautiful demonstrations of how people spoke with God and how God responded to them. For our purposes here we will use a section of Psalm 143 where the writer models quite well the progression of moving from his own thoughts to hearing from God.

> "I remember the days of old, I think about your deeds. I meditate on the works of your hands. I stretch out my hands to you; my soul thirsts for you like a parched land. Answer me quickly, O Lord...let me hear of your steadfast love in the morning. Teach me the way I should go, for to you I lift up my soul. Teach me to do your will, for you are my God. Let your good Spirit lead me on a level path" (Ps.143:5-8, 10).

The first thing we notice here is the Psalmist's act of focusing. "I remember the days of old, I think about your deeds, I meditate on the works of your hands." He has deliberately turned his thoughts toward some works of God that he already knows about and for which he is truly grateful. These are not fleeting thoughts, but things he spends time considering and reflecting on. He allows himself to feel genuine gratitude while reflecting, and by doing so, he engages his entire heart and mind in the process.

What follows is a stirring of his heart: "I stretch out my hands to you; my soul thirsts for you like a parched land." He allows himself to get caught up in the feelings of desire that he has for God, and expresses himself freely.

His desire quickly becomes a prayer to connect and hear God's heart: "Let me hear of your steadfast love in the morning." Finally, he expresses his desire and willingness to be mentored by God. In effect he is saying, "Show me whatever it is I need to know for this day."

The great thing about this Psalm is the way the psalmist begins with where he is at that moment in time – what he knows, and what he remembers of God's goodness – and ends up in touch with the cry of his heart and his need for more of God's light in his life. Focusing and reflecting on God opens a doorway to a heart-to-heart connection that creates a desire to be mentored in the ways of the Kingdom.

This is why learning how to immerse ourselves in spiritual reflection is so important. By ruminating on a verse, an idea, or a life issue for a while in the presence of God, we prepare ourselves to see and hear what he wants to reveal to us. Let's slow this process down a bit more and look at some of the nuances of spiritual reflection.

What We Mean by "Reflection"

As we transition to a receptive, listening state, we need to clarify what is meant by *spiritual reflection*. This is important, because very few of us have been taught how to spend time reflecting in ways that are life-giving.

For example, let's say I decide to reflect on God's faithfulness to me. One way is to view this like a mental challenge to see how many biblical events I can name that capture this idea. I might even think of it as getting the right answer to a Bible quiz. That may help me feel smart, but it probably will not do much for my heart. Unfortunately, this is what most of us have learned to think of as reflecting on God's Word.

But suppose I approach this another way entirely. Very quietly, I allow some of God's greatest interventions in my own life to come to mind one at a time and savor the meaning and impact of each one for a while before looking for another. As I consider them, I let myself feel wonder about this God who moved heaven and earth in such amazing ways to bring me to himself.

You can see how this is a very different way of reflecting than just relying on my raw intellectual effort and rational analysis. In this way we are more prepared to allow our perceptions to arise from our heart rather than to work them out by brainpower alone. Instead of trying to master a subject, we allow ourselves to be led through it, making observations along the way about its nature and significance, and noticing our own internal reactions as well. We may feel led to ask questions about the issue at hand, or make connections to various other Scriptures or events in our life. As our thoughts progress, they tend to become more exploratory in nature and we become more receptive to receiving thoughts and images from God.

When the psalmist in the previous passage begins to feel drawn to God and his emotions are stirred, he gives those feelings a voice and expresses the desires of his heart. With almost the simplicity of a child, he tells God how much he wants to be with him and how much he needs him. This transparency and freedom of heart is an important part of bonding with God, allowing ourselves to enjoy his wonder and grace and love.

Continuing on in the psalm, we arrive at the point where the writer is passionately desiring to hear from God and is highly receptive. So he begins to ask God to give him what he needs to know. One of the most important questions we can ask God is, "What else can you tell me about this?" or "What am I missing?" because his ways are higher than our ways (Isa.55:8-9) and we are always in need of something more than what we have. Asking God to teach us is not an imposition on him or some kind of self-centered request but exactly the sort of response to him that he is waiting for. God wants to train up his children in his ways.[6] The more teachable we are, the more we can receive from him.

---

[6] "The Spirit will teach you all things" (Jn.14:26).

Moving from Impressions to Concrete Words

Quite often when we receive impressions from God, we sense them with our spirit but do not immediately have words that can express well what we are experiencing. We have only a strong awareness that God is showing us something important. Sometimes this feels like a thought that is not yet fully formed, an idea we are still reaching for. In this way our heart can lead our mind, and as we allow the impression to be fleshed out we will find the necessary words and pictures that make sense of that impression.

For example, Chapter Two includes a reflection in which I decided to ask the question, "What are the roots of my reluctance?" Almost as soon as I wrote it down, I had a strong impression of something being turned inside out, and immediately knew that the question I had just written was missing the point. A second later a new question came to mind, "When have I *not* been reluctant?" That statement gave substance to the impression I had just experienced. Writing it out felt like a revelation, following which, my mind began to be flooded with memories of costly commitments in my past. It was as if a doorway had opened to an entire room full of reasons why I might be reluctant to engage with God.

In retrospect, my spirit knew that the first question was "inside out" even before my mind thought it through. When I noticed this internal reaction, I kept my focus there until I understood what it was that I needed to say out loud and write down. That led to what God wanted to show me about my reluctance.

This way of receiving an impression is quite common. God will speak to us in a way that our heart begins to grasp even before we have the words for what he is showing us. As we hold those impressions and pursue them for a few moments, the words begin to come that do justice to what our spirit is hearing.

It is important in this process that we finish these thoughts and not leave them in the form of vague abstractions. Impressions we have about God's heart in a matter, about the meaning of something important, or anything else that comes to mind during our reflection needs to be verbalized in whatever words best capture the thought.

Usually that means either speaking the words out loud or writing them down. Since most of us do not have the discipline to hold a single train of thought for any extended time without getting distracted in some way, writing out our conversations with God or speaking them out loud to God helps us to focus and even heighten our grasp of the things we are considering. Insights we receive are better anchored in the soul when we verbalize them, and any mistaken thoughts we may have are more easily discerned when we put them into concrete terms.

My own preference is to write out my conversations with God, often in complete sentences. In addition to keeping me focused, this approach to reflecting provides a number of significant benefits. For one thing, I literally *see* what I'm thinking and that provides another avenue of feedback for my mind. Once it is on the page I can question it, discern whether I am going in a helpful direction, and make better choices about how to proceed.

Sometimes I look at what I have written and know immediately that the words fail to capture what I believe God is trying to tell me. So I jot a note next to my first attempt and try again. If I am captured by another thought that seems more pressing, I can switch gears without worrying about whether I will lose what I have received up to that point on the current matter, because I can always look at what I wrote earlier.

When I come back the next day, I do not have to try to remember what I was talking to God about or whether any of that needs to be addressed further. Rereading my previous entry almost always helps me quiet and focus for my time with God and helps to provide continuity to his mentoring from one day to the next.

When I do talk to God while hiking or pacing around, I usually take along a notepad so I can jot down the significant elements that come to mind and not forget them. If I just let myself drift from one impression to another without verbalizing them at all, I usually come away dissatisfied with my connection or forget half of what went through my mind.

The point is that we need to "translate" our impressions into words and capture them in some way so they do not lose their impact, and to make it easier for us to discern whether they are from God.

Summary

Listening to God is not at all a passive act. We do not empty our mind and wait for some thought to strike us out of nowhere. It is a conversation that has all the elements of meaningful spiritual reflection coupled with the expectation that God will meet us, teach us, guide us, and reveal himself to us.

And while this is not passive, neither do we approach our conversation with the intention of demonstrating mastery over whatever it is we are considering. Instead, we actively engage as an apprentice in need of a mentor. We come with a searching heart, submitting to the process of being shaped by God and longing for more of his love and presence in our life.

Finally, reflecting and receiving are very experiential and not just cerebral. We engage with God with all our mind and soul – our thoughts, hopes and fears, our deepest secrets, and our loftiest desires. And we do all of this with as much trust as we can find, believing that as we expose ourself to God he will reveal himself to us. Within that space, we will find a God who loves us dearly and offers us life.

DISCERNING

Given that God truly wants to connect with us and talk to us, and given that it is possible for us to slow down enough to receive from him what he wants to communicate to us, we come naturally to the next area of concern: *How do we know that we are actually following his lead, that our thoughts are really being illuminated by the Spirit of God, and that we are not being led astray in this process?* Clearly, we need some discernment to have conversations with God.

There is a lot more to this than just being right. Knowing that God is speaking to us in a given moment is reassuring to our soul. It tells us that we are on his heart, that we matter to God himself. We can drink in his words to us, receiving them deep into our soul, and revel in the life they create in us. Consider how different our experience would be from that, if we are wondering whether we can believe what we are hearing, or whether God is saying anything to us at all. That is why discernment is so important.

For example, in Chapter One I included a reflection on Psalm 23 in which I visualized an overflowing cup. When I "backed away" from the cup in my mind's eye, I saw Jesus pouring into the cup and thoroughly enjoying the mess that he was making. Now one obvious question is, "Was that my own imagination or was I being led by God?" We really want to be able to tell the difference. Otherwise, who knows where we might end up? As we take a closer look at discernment, I will refer back to this reflection from time to time to see if we can make sense of what I saw there.

The Difference Between Discerning and Censoring

When most of us hear the word "discernment" we tend to think in terms of the ability to *evaluate* whether something is good or bad, or the wisdom to know what to do about something.

Those are certainly important aspects of discernment. But we also need to consider *the reasons behind* our efforts to discern.

I have seen some people who are so concerned about the possibility of having an errant thought sneak into their mind that they miss many of the gems that are right in front of them. Their fear keeps them from seeing much of what God wants to show them, all the while thinking that they are being careful by "discerning." Such approaches to listening can easily turn our conversations with God into highly stressful events instead of the life-giving experiences they are meant to be.

Discerning is first and foremost an act of noticing or observing. When I saw Jesus pouring wine into a cup that was already overflowing, I immediately began to notice a few things. First, I noticed how odd the scene was – this is not how we normally expect people to act when they have poured too much into a cup. Then I became aware of my own delight at the sight of it, and how much Jesus seemed to be enjoying himself. As those observations became conscious thoughts, I also noticed my heart leaping for joy. All of this occurred in a matter of seconds.

Now what is important here is that these observations are a critical part of determining whether these images were coming from God or whether my own sense of humor was running away with the scene. The reason why these observations are so important is that we cannot evaluate what we have not noticed.

We can become so overly-focused on whether our last thought was theologically sound that we can lose sight of the process itself, our relationship to God, or our internal reactions to what is happening. Often Christians are so afraid of hearing something from the enemy or of giving too much validity to their own thoughts that they effectively censor their impressions before the thoughts even take shape. Unless it sounds like something right out of the Bible, they fret over every thought and scrutinize each one for any hint of the flesh, lest they mistake something to be God's voice when it is not.

Suppose my initial thought had been, "This can't be right since Jesus never made a mess except that time when he was mad at the money-changers in the Temple." That would probably have shut down the whole scene and robbed me of what was about to happen. Although my intent might have been to avoid making any mistakes in my listening, this kind of hyper-vigilance would have actually made hearing from God more difficult.

Our conversations with God are meant to be life-giving and soul-filling. How is that possible if we spend all of our time worrying about what might go wrong? *It is very hard to build trust in God when our approach to connecting with him is rooted and steeped in fear.* That is enough to get in the way of hearing anything at all. We need to find a way of discerning that is not so fear-based.

While these concerns may come from a well-meaning attempt to keep us from error, they actually do not hold up very well under close examination. Among other things, viewing this listening process through the lens of "right and wrong" is itself a questionable process. If we were to be perfectly honest, poor thoughts run through our mind all the time – from contempt to hate and from pride to self-pity. Why do we think all of our thoughts suddenly have to be perfect just because we are talking to God?

Maybe we are trying to impress God with how good we are. Or perhaps we are afraid that unless we are really careful, the enemy will deceive us and we will go off in some bad direction. Either way, we would do much better to relax a little and simply acknowledge that we are shot through with flaws, that our mind can be very unruly, that our passions may not yet be tamed, and that we need to come to God just as we are in order to deal honestly with this issue of hearing well.

Of course we will have unwanted thoughts intrude on our time with God! We will probably put words in his mouth that he did not say. We may even follow in the footsteps of Peter for a while and blurt out things that are way off base. That is just part of our learning process. This is *not* a performance test! We are merely apprentices, learning how to live in the Kingdom one step at a time. Our task is not to get the conversation perfectly, but to *pay attention* to what is going on and take everything back to God, asking him to show us what we need to know.

There is absolutely nothing wrong with writing a paragraph in your journal and then *noticing* that it has no life in it or that it does not sound right. When you stop to ask God what that is about, he may quite possibly confirm your suspicion that those words did not go in the direction you need to go. So you make a note like, "(something missing here)" and ask God what he wants you to know, and start again. This is how we learn.

Writing out our faulty ideas on paper where they can be seen for what they really are can actually be quite valuable. God is so much bigger than our mistaken ideas and halting steps. We honestly *do not* need to be afraid of putting down the wrong words or hearing something from our own mind when we think we are listening to God. Nor do we need to feel condemned if we get things wrong. God knows we are still in training.

What *is* important is that we stay teachable, knowing we are engaged in a life-long apprenticeship. A little humility goes a long way to aid our discernment, because it helps us notice when things are out of sync. Ironically, the more we try to quote God or worry about getting everything right, the harder it is to really discern what we have "received" and the less receptive we will be in regard to revising the faulty thoughts we already have.

I hope this is liberating. Having thoughts that we trust at first but then correct or improve on in later conversations with the

Spirit is not a problem for either us or God. As we pay attention to the promptings of the Spirit, he will help us make the necessary course corrections as needed. At times we may even need to seek help from a trusted friend who can help us separate things out. But the principle remains the same – we are always learning, and that's a good thing, not an indictment on our lack of perfection.

My intent here is to emphasize how safe it is to be an imperfect being in the hands of a perfect God who loves us as much as he does. Learning how to discern his voice is just one more thing at which we can be imperfect. We can rejoice in his gift of speaking to us and become more like him by spending time with him without worrying about getting it all "right." As long as we stay teachable, God will get us to where we need to go in our understanding.

So having established that we need a lot of grace in our conversations and that we do not need to be fearful of having thoughts that are not from God or guided by God, we still need to go back to the question of how to tell the difference. After all, we do want to know when God is leading us. To address this, we will consider the issue of discernment from two vantage points – discerning the *process* we are involved in as we talk with God, and discerning the *content* of what comes to mind during our conversation.

Discerning the Process

Discerning the process is mostly about *noticing how we are proceeding* with the other three aspects of conversational prayer. It is like having a radar running in the background that is continually taking stock of what is going on. If we slow it down to a snail's pace, watching the process might be viewed as a set of questions that we use to check on the nature and quality of our conversation.

In the area of Focusing:

> Am I being distracted by external noise?
> Am I honestly expecting to receive something from God?
> Am I paying attention to my reactions?

In the area of Listening:

> Do these words capture my impressions well enough?
> Do I need to "shift gears" and try something else?
> Is there a better question I can ask?

In the area of Responding:

> Do I need to stop and respond to what I have received so far?
> Am I at the point where I need to close?
> How can I hold on to what I have received during this time?

The reason we need to consider these kinds of questions is because it is so easy to become distracted, drift off topic, run out of steam, depend too much on our prior information instead of receiving from God, become too analytical, trivialize important things, emphasize non-important things, and so on. Discernment helps us stay on course.

Now in practice if we stopped to ask all these questions every other minute, we would probably end up being so distracted with discernment itself that we would never get around to listening. Discernment is not a grid that everything must pass through, but rather a *mindset* that aids us in hearing well from God. It is a way of sensing and paying attention to whatever is going through our mind and body, and testing the path that we are on to see which way to go.

Discerning the process often feels a bit like walking along in a fog, from time to time checking the walkway under our feet to see that we are still going in the right direction and feeling our way along so as not to get lost. If I remain sensitive to any changes in my mood or thought I will notice things that help me see where I am, and I will then be able to respond accordingly or check in with God if I am not sure what to do next.

Once again, a little humility can be a great asset in this process. Because we are fallible human beings, we must be willing to learn as we go and keep in mind that we are always apprentices not only of whatever the Spirit wants to teach us, but also in regard to *learning how to learn* and learning how to sense what it is like for God's Spirit to communicate with our spirit.

A good example of discerning the process can be seen in my experience with Psalm 23. As I contemplated the image of a goblet bubbling up like a fountain, I gradually became aware of an uneasy feeling that something was not quite right with the picture. My response to this awareness was that I needed to see more of what I was missing. So I backed away from the scene, largely by going back to the text in my mind and recalling that it says God is the one who is preparing the table and doing all these things. As I took in the bigger picture, I saw Jesus pouring the wine.

Initially, it had seemed good to reflect on the image of an overflowing cup. After all, that represents abundance. But at the point when I became aware of something nagging at the edges of my mind, I first needed to notice that something was out of place and then make a decision about shifting my focus in another way. As it turned out, my decision to back away from the scene proved to be what I needed in order to receive more from this interaction. Had that not been the case, I simply would have looked for something else.

Let me emphasize here that the choices about what to do with our observations are not merely guesses or random efforts, nor are they solutions worked out through logic and reason. To the best of our ability to follow, our choices must be guided just like the rest of the process. Everything is wrapped up in our relationship with God and our awareness of his presence with us in conversation. My decision to back away from the scene was only partly a conscious choice. It was really more of a yielding to the inner promptings I sensed from looking back at the text.

Throughout our time of reflecting and talking with God we will usually explore a number of avenues, sometimes searching our memory for any place that seems connected to what we are discussing, sometimes searching our emotional responses for clues to internal issues we may not be aware of, and sometimes giving expression to the promptings of the Spirit. In all of this we want to be sensitive to God's leading, always moving toward whatever he is drawing us to, and learning to follow his lead.

Discerning the Content

In addition to discerning the *process* that we are involved in, we must also learn how to discern the *content* of what we are writing down or speaking out as things come to mind. Making sense of the impressions we receive from God is something we learn experientially over time.

One thing in particular we need to be very clear about is that expressing our own thoughts regarding a matter is an important aspect of any conversation with God. That is simply our part in being an active apprentice. The Psalms are full of this kind of writing, and through them we benefit greatly by hearing the joys and struggles of those who have gone before us. Many of them wrestled with hard questions about where God was in difficult times and wrote out their thoughts and prayers, or rejoiced when they saw the hand of God in their life.

Just because our thoughts are not God's thoughts does not mean there is no value to getting them out on the table. To take stock of how we are doing with life is to be deliberate about our journey. Writing out our deepest thoughts can go a long way toward helping us become consciously aware of what is going on inside us. Hearing and writing down our own thoughts is not something to be afraid of doing while trying to hear God. It is simply our part of the conversation, and can actually be a very important prelude to hearing how God sees our heart and mind as well as the issue at hand. Not everything that goes through our mind needs to be God's voice in order to be helpful in this process.

Still, if I am discerning the content, it means that I am generally aware when the things I am verbalizing are mostly my own thoughts and to what extent they seem to be led by the Spirit of God. The truth is, for most people most of the time, the majority of what goes through our mind during conversational prayer is our own reflective thinking and remembering, even when the direction of our thoughts is guided by the Holy Spirit. Such thoughts often help us to focus and even discern where we want to go with the conversation. They may even be edifying in and of themselves, such as when we take time to remember the good things God has done for us and allow those feelings of gratitude to flourish for a while.

But how do we know when our thoughts are coming from God? Again, God's thoughts and words have an inherent quality about them that makes them different, due to several divine characteristics which they possess.

One of the amazing things about God's voice is that it carries the power of life (Jn.6:63). A friend can tell me something I need to hear, yet his words may have very little effect on me because they are just words. But when God says those very same things to me, his words can change my life. When we hear God clearly, his words can go deep into our heart and mind, changing our soul in ways that we cannot manage to do on our own.

For example, I know a man who lived under some very heavy condemnation for many years regarding the mistakes he made in parenting his children. No matter what his friends told him or what he tried to tell himself, he felt as if the things he had done and left undone were very nearly unforgivable. One day while talking to God about this, he heard God tell him he was forgiven. Only then did he finally experience relief from the guilt and shame he had carried around for so long. God's voice penetrated his heart in a way that no other voice could ever reach.

God's words to us also have a quality of grace about them that is richer and deeper than human words. Even when he confronts us, he does it in a way that communicates his care for us and his desire to walk with us through our healing. Sometimes he uses humor. Other times we may feel his tenderness in the very words he uses, or we may feel his arms around us as he tells us what we need to hear. But the kindness of his heart for us will usually be very evident. And that is one of the ways we will know that it is God who is bringing up the confrontation.

During one of my spiritual dry spells I felt compelled to ask God what he thought about me neglecting our time together. Although I really expected him to give me a stern lecture about how inconsistent I was and how I should really know better by now, and so on, what he said to me was simply, "I really miss you." Instantly, my heart softened, my soul opened up to his love, and whatever resistance I still harbored completely vanished. One might call that a confrontation, but there was not an ounce of condemnation anywhere near it. He knows how to give us the redirection we need without beating us over the head.

Another characteristic of God speaking to us is that he will often say things we would not have thought of on our own. The words we hear will be phrased in a way that is different from our normal pattern of thinking, a kind of perspective we would not otherwise have. In every way they are qualitatively better than our normal thoughts (Isa.55:8-9).

Perhaps the single most telling evidence that God has spoken into our spirit is the fruit that it bears. Often we experience the value of it even as the impressions are taking shape. We may feel a peace or an awe that seems to cover our whole being. We may experience an instant burst of excitement or joy that makes us want to dance around the room or break into thanksgiving. At times an insight can be so freeing that it feels like someone turned on a light in the room or lifted a sixty-pound weight off our shoulders. When this happens we can be fairly certain that we have received something from God.

Given that God is the sole author of life, an experience of life-giving fruit is a tremendously strong indicator that God is involved. In fact a good rule of thumb is that *the more life-giving an insight or experience is, the more you can be sure that it came from God.*

Sometimes the fruit takes a while to become visible. We wake up one day and notice that our attitudes have changed about something or our expectations of God or life are different than they were a few months ago.

After one particularly painful encounter with God in which I believe he revealed and healed a major source of my self-hate, I noticed a complete change of heart about my personal failures and I stopped beating myself up. At first I was a little skeptical that this life-long pattern could really be broken. But after several months, the long-term fruit was proof to me that he had truly healed something very significant in that encounter. I could then say with confidence that I had heard from him in that experience and had not just talked myself out of a bad mood.

Over time, we will experience a growing trust in God's heart for us, while our fear of his disapproval or his expectations of us will diminish. We will find ourselves desiring more of what he wants for us and wanting a lot less of whatever the world has to offer.

Taking notice of these various elements that point to God's involvement is an important part of learning to hear God's voice. As we reflect on whatever fruit of goodness is evident in our life, we can bring together in our mind and heart the revelations we have received and the fruit that resulted, both short term and long term. That way the next time we have a similar encounter we will be more equipped to recognize the ways in which God speaks to us. As we become more accustomed to these kinds of interactions with him, we will grow to be more sensitive to the nuances of his Spirit speaking into our life.

RESPONDING

Spending focused time with God is life-giving in and of itself, and receiving life from him is reason enough to engage with him. But there is even more. If we then deliberately respond in meaningful ways to what we have been given, his truth and love will penetrate even more deeply into our soul.

Throughout our time of conversational prayer there are usually many opportunities to respond to his leading. Each prompting and response leads us deeper into communion with God. And as our focused time draws to a close, it is especially important to look for ways we can respond to the goodness of God we have received, so that we internalize our experience of him more concretely.

Sometimes the insights we receive in our conversations are so powerful that they replace mistaken ideas we have about life, about God, or about our own identity almost instantaneously. In that case our response may very naturally be one of gratitude and thanksgiving, arising spontaneously from the freedom we feel. Allowing gratitude to well up in our heart and stay there for a while is a way of "beholding the beauty of the Lord" (Ps.27) and strengthening our relationship with God.

Other times we may want to be more deliberate about our response and give as much care to that as the process of listening itself. As with every other aspect of conversational prayer, *how to respond* is something we can ask God about. Either way, the kinds of questions we would want to address at this time are:

What do I want to take with me from this time?

What do I *need* to take with me?

How can I hold on to these gifts or these insights?

What do I want to come back to again and discuss further?

Quite often we will find that one of the other forms of prayer provides just what we need to capture the heart of our time together. For example, if our time with God reveals things in our heart that we were either unaware of or had been pushing aside for some reason, we may feel moved to a prayer of repentance or renunciation as part of our desire to be free of these things.

A particularly powerful but often neglected way of responding to God is to simply *be with him*, quietly, to "be still and know" that he is God (Ps.46:10). In our busy world we may be prone to say of our conversation with God, "That was nice" and rush on to the next thing in our agenda for the day. But when we experience the presence of God in some significant way during out time together, or if we have a really strong sense of his love for us, his goodness, his faithfulness to our restoration, or some other aspect of his character, one of the most important things we can do in that moment is to be still and enjoy him and his presence with us.

Conversations with God can also stir us to action. We may feel led to contact someone and get together with them. We may feel led to offer amends to someone we have hurt, to ask forgiveness, or to forgive. And because our God is such a giving God, we can feel moved to give some of our time or resources to others, or to offer something to someone in a way that may encourage them or lift them up.

Taking a few moments to deliberately *respond* in some way to our time with God helps us to anchor those thoughts and insights in our body and mind. When our time with God is particularly fruitful, we will often respond spontaneously, without much need to think about what to do. Other times we may want to brainstorm for a few minutes or ask God what would be most helpful. And if for some reason we have not received much during our time, we may respond by simply writing down some things we would like to return to at a later date.

LET'S PRACTICE!

Conversational prayer is something you can continue to grow into for the rest of your life. You can always go deeper in your conversations with God. But the truth is, you probably already know enough at this point to begin! Remember, this is not something that you have to get "right." Conversations with God are part of having a genuine relationship with him, not a test to see how well you do. Enjoy it!

Lord God, I want more than anything to be closer to You right now. Help me open my heart to You and to know how close You really are. Let me receive whatever You have for me. Help me to hear whatever You say and to see whatever You want to reveal. Lead me now as we spend this time together. In Jesus' name....

PERSONAL REFLECTION

Does this sound like something you can incorporate into your life?
Is this something you are willing to make time for?
If so, how do you plan to organize your time to include this in
your daily or weekly schedule?

DISCUSSION QUESTIONS

How do you quiet yourself when you are upset? What works well?
What about this way of engaging with God is most intriguing to
you? What reservations do you still have?

EXERCISE

Our goal for this exercise is to explore how much God loves us
and how important it is to grasp this in our spirit. We begin with
an amazing little parcel of Paul's prayer for the saints in Ephesus:

> "And I pray that you, being rooted and established in love,
> may have power, together with all the saints, to grasp how
> wide and long and high and deep is the love of Christ, and to
> know this love that surpasses knowledge" (Eph.3:17-19).

The first thing I want you to do is allow yourself to believe that
this passage holds a lot of treasures that are not immediately
apparent. Accept that by faith the Holy Spirit can open your heart
to the wonder and beauty of this prayer. Please do not skim
through the rest of this just to see what the exercise looks like and
move on, as its value to you can only be seen and known as you
experience it.

Give yourself at least a half an hour for this exercise. Take each
of the following steps, one at a time, spending some time in each

one. I have deliberately broken it down into bite-size pieces in order to help you move through your time with God in as thoughtful a manner as possible.

- Ask God to persuade your heart to slow down and take this in slowly and deliberately.

- Imagine Paul writing with all his passion and desire to help his readers see how amazing this love is that he wants them to know experientially.

- Read the passage slowly, letting its breadth and depth flow over your heart and mind. Read it again, looking for more depth.

- Look for a word or phrase that really captures your interest or imagination.

- Begin writing to God about that word/phrase. Lay out before him what you feel about it, how you were drawn to it, and why it has your attention.

- Let him intensify your interest and ask him to improve your focus.

- Keep writing as your spirit yearns to grasp what God's Spirit is revealing to you. Ask him what you need to know about it.

- Let him know how you feel about what he is giving you.

- When you reach a point where you feel as if this reflection is beginning to run its course, go back over what you have written, seeking to be led even deeper into what God is showing you. Begin writing again whenever you feel re-inspired to continue.

- Take a break from writing for responding as needed.

- Ask God to help you summarize what he has shown you.

- Ask him how to best hold on to what he has shown you.

- Spend some time in appreciation to him for your time together.

MORE IDEAS

We have only begun to scratch the surface of how God wants to minister to you and reveal his Word to you. But as you already know if you have tried to read the Bible before, Scripture can vary quite a lot in terms of how it impacts us. For that reason I would like to suggest that you begin with some passages I have found to be so full of life that I have gone back to them many times. Nearly every phrase is filled with food for your soul. Take them slow and spend enough time with them to allow the Spirit to make them real to you. I also have included a list of individual verses in the Addendum that I have found to be really full of life – please check them out.

Remember that the key to this is to take the passages very slowly. Reach for depth. Each phrase can be an entire conversation with God, so do not hurry through them. May God richly bless you as you ponder these words.

Isaiah 55
Psalm 23, 27, 84, 100, and 139
John 14-17
Ephesians 1-4
Colossians 1-3

Chapter 4 – How Writing Can Help

"Write all the words which I have spoken to you in a book" (Jer.30:2).

Recently a friend of mine told me – in a very excited tone of voice – that while she had been listening to God for some time, she had only recently begun to write out her conversations on paper. To her surprise, she found herself going much deeper, hearing much more clearly, and receiving much more life from her conversations than ever before.

Her experience echos mine, as well as that of many others I have spoken to. Writing out our reflections or even jotting down notes as we go along in our conversations can have a tremendous impact on our ability to hear, discern and internalize the things that God is wanting to reveal to us.

I would not be at all surprised if some of you are seriously considering whether to skip this chapter. You may have little to no desire to write down anything about your inner life. Perhaps it feels too much like doing homework, or something about having it in print makes you feel vulnerable.

Please hear me out. This is not just about making a record of your conversations, although that actually does have a lot of value. Nor is it simply busy work. The main reason for keeping a journal is that when used well, it becomes a valuable tool to help you focus better, hear better and discern better.

Even if you do not like writing or have some other reason why you would rather not write down your thoughts as you talk to God, please consider seriously the suggestions in this chapter. The benefits of a journal will far outweigh any discomfort or effort you may experience in learning how to use one. And for those of you who decide in the end not to keep such a journal, the thoughts presented here are still important and will be helpful as you engage with God in your own way.

Why Journal?

One of the most important reasons to write out your conversations with God is that it requires a lot more focus than contemplation alone. The discipline of moving all of your reflections to the point of concrete words on a page requires deliberate engagement of your attention and full use of your mind in order to process all of the impressions, images and emotions through the medium of language. That, in turn, helps you to find deeper meaning in the things that God is drawing you toward. Without specific words, our ideas and impressions can easily become a mental fog with very little sense of direction or purpose.

Capturing our ideas in concrete terms also improves our discernment, as we then have very specific words to work with instead of vague notions. Once our thoughts are down on paper, we may have reactions to them that we would not have experienced had our thoughts remained less defined. In some cases, our words will even expose some of the faulty premises we believe deep inside or various intentions of our heart that need God's touch. On the other hand, when the thoughts are from God, putting them into words can hit us with all the force of a revelation. Having them on paper allows us to return to them over and over in the days ahead, and to let the Spirit work them into our heart.

Another reason to write out our conversation with God is to slow our thoughts down and process things more deliberately. Research is beginning to show us that the internet and cell phone age is impacting how we think, contributing significantly to distracted thought patterns and shorter attention spans. But deep spiritual reflection requires quiet, focused attention for extended periods of time. Writing out our conversations by hand helps us to slow down, to focus more intently, and to reflect more deeply than most other forms of communication we practice from day to day.

For those who really hate to write or are reluctant to keep a journal, I would encourage you to experiment with this for a while to see its impact on your prayer life. If after a few weeks you still find this to be more distracting than helpful, then try your conversational prayer without it and see if that works any better. Even then I would suggest that you have your conversations with God out loud, so that you translate your impressions into concrete terms. When you have an important insight, at least write that much down so that you do not lose track of the gifts God has given you over time.

Keeping Your Journal

Here are the basic mechanics of keeping a journal.

1. Date each entry.
2. After asking God to open your heart and mind to his voice, read the previous entry from your journal.
3. Discern whether to continue the train of thought from the previous entry or to move on to something else.
4. If moving on to another area, discern whether you want to work from a Biblical text, discuss a life issue, or simply spend time with God.
5. Begin writing your thoughts, impressions, questions, reactions, feelings, discernment, and prayers.

6. As you write, highlight items that seem particularly significant by underlining, using all capital letters, or making stars or other notations around the words that are meaningful to you.
7. Write down the ways you feel led to respond. Write out your prayers.

Throughout your conversation, be willing to search for the words that best capture your impressions. Feel free to use whatever writing style works best for you. Some people use full sentences as much as possible, while others only jot down the most significant ideas they have. The point is for the act of writing to become a way of bringing more focus to your thoughts and impressions. Writing too much may distract some people, while writing too little may keep others from sufficiently engaging.

Do not worry about how well you write – this is for your eyes only. Let your thoughts flow to the paper, expressing the desires and impressions of your heart. Write with abandon.

Be willing to include any discernment about your process and content as well, so as not to censor your thoughts (although if you see that your mind is wandering, you do not need to write out the content of your "rabbit trail"). Be aware that some impressions may take a while to form themselves into words. Allow the words to come to you and do not force them. Other than that, follow the guidelines described in the previous chapter.

I would also discourage the use of a computer for journaling, because the act of writing by hand is much more creative and flexible. By using a pen I can change my style to match my mood, sketch out diagrams, and add stuff in the margins almost without effort. Those same actions on a keyboard are distracting and cumbersome. Writing by hand also moves things through our mind differently and changes how we focus, which is very important in this high-tech age we live in.

Using Your Journal

While everyone develops their own way of organizing and utilizing their journal, I would like to offer a few suggestions to get you started so that you do not have to reinvent everything for yourself.

First, I would suggest keeping a few pages at the very beginning or end of your journal for special things such as:

People – a list of people to pray for.

Issues – a list of things you would like to talk to God about but have not done so yet.

Index – a list (by date) of especially important insights or healings that you want to be able to find again.

Often ideas will come to mind during your conversations that you would love to pursue, but they are not connected to the current topic. One approach is to discern whether to stay with the current train of thought or move to the new idea, and then make a note in your "Issues" list of whichever area you are putting aside. You are then certain of being able to return to the deferred theme at a later date, and can give your full attention to the one at hand without worrying about forgetting the other.

I would also suggest making good use of the margins in your journal. Use them to "star" particularly important insights or to identify recurring themes. For example, God has really placed on my heart the last few years the theme of "Abiding in Him." That is a phrase we hear from time to time in our churches. But to be perfectly honest, there is precious little practical help or teaching regarding how this actually looks. So whenever my conversations with God touch on issues that would help expand either my understanding or my experience of abiding in Christ, I write the word "Abiding" in the margin. Anytime I want to go back over what God has taught me about abiding, all I need to do is scan my previous journals for "Abiding" in the margin and put the pieces together.

I also use the margins for some of my discernment notations. Sometimes as I write my thoughts out it becomes clear to me that they are leading me away from where I need to go. So I draw a bracket around them in the margin area and make a note like, "No! Need to go another way" and then drop down a few lines and start again.

Speaking of skipping lines, I highly recommend leaving a blank line whenever your thoughts take a significant change in direction. That way if you want to return to your earlier thought, it is very easy to see where you left off. When you read your journal at a later date you will be able to anticipate the changes as you read. Otherwise, you may be halfway into the next sentence before you realize that the focus has changed.

I also like to put a title at the beginning of each entry. When I am asking God to open up a verse or phrase of Scripture, I use the reference for a heading and then write out the text underneath before skipping a line and starting my own thoughts. If I am talking to God about a life issue, I usually put an abbreviated subject line on top, like "More Family Stuff" or "Feeling Really Stressed." That way if I want to come back in a few days to see what I wrote, I can find it quite easily.

When you finish one journal and begin another, be sure to write on the cover the date-range of the entries it contains. Someday you will have a stack of journals, and you will want to be able to set them in some kind of order.

Summary

Next to conversational prayer itself, keeping a journal has been one of the most valuable practices in which I have ever engaged. Nothing helps me focus as well or discern so much of what God is giving me. My prayer for you is that you will find it as helpful as I have.

Lord, I pray that You will deeply bless our times together. I pray that Your words will be life to me and Your presence will be food for my soul. Help me write down those things You give me in a way that will make it possible to come back to them and be nourished again at a later time. Thank You. In Jesus' name...

PERSONAL REFLECTION

How long would you be willing to experiment with a journal to see how well it works for you?

DISCUSSION QUESTIONS

What experiences have you had with any form of journaling in the past? In what ways have they been helpful or discouraging?

EXERCISE

Get a blank journal.

Plan a short retreat (1-2 hours)

- Choose a location.
- Choose a passage and/or an issue.
- Spend time seeking God's presence.
- Spend time writing out your reflections and listening to God.

Part 2 – Going Deeper

For those who would like to know more about conversational prayer, and for those who need more help in how to have these conversations with God, the rest of this book is intended to provide additional direction.

Chapter 5 – Focusing

More about quieting our soul and focusing on God.

Chapter 6 – Listening

More about paying attention to the promptings and revelations of the Spirit.

Chapter 7 – Discerning

More about noticing the content and process of our conversations with God.

Chapter 8 – Responding

More about responding to what we are receiving.

Chapter 9 – When Hearing God is Difficult

Addressing special problems that interfere with our conversations.

Chapter 10 – Reaping the Rewards

Another look at the benefits of conversational prayer.

Chapter 5 – Focusing

"Be still and know that I am God" (Ps.46:10).

"To gaze upon the beauty of the Lord" (Ps.27:4).

When we turn the eyes of our heart to see what cannot otherwise be seen, when we stop to listen to what only our soul can hear, an amazingly beautiful world awaits for us to discover and uncover the treasures that it holds. God's love for us is so vast and so wide that his very presence with us is food for our soul. And every encounter is ripe with new life that draws us closer to himself, infuses us with hope, and makes us more into the people he has designed us to be.

This is why we long to spend time with him. Even if we never heard a single word or phrase, just the joy of being with him would be incentive enough to quiet our heart and focus on God.

We need to keep in mind that focusing is an intentional act on our part to respond to God. Although he is in us and with us all the time, God rarely forces himself on our conscious awareness. If we want to be aware of his presence and hear him speak into our life, we need to turn toward him consciously and deliberately.

Focusing on God means that we set aside time to meet with him and then guard that time as we would any meeting with a friend or beloved mentor. Within the space that we make to meet with God, we must be quite intentional about bringing our thoughts into focus and engaging God with our whole mind. Because this is so important, we will now address some of the unique challenges to this aspect of conversational prayer.

Taking Time for Our Relationship With God

One of the most common problems we have with conversational prayer is simply the time that it takes. We are busy people with busy schedules. Taking time out of our day for talking to God or reflecting on a verse can feel like trying to hold the lid on a steaming pot. Every minute we spend with God means more pressure on the rest of our day.

Without meaning to, we can easily focus on the static in our mind and drown out the still small voice of the Spirit. As we feel the moment slipping away, the prospect of needing even more time to quiet down can make us even more anxious. We may be tempted to just give up and move on with our day, unable to quiet long enough in order to connect well with God.

Many of us are over-extended, and every new demand on our time creates a kind of inner dread or feeling of exhaustion. Adding something to our daily or weekly routine seems impossible. Prayer can easily be seen as too "non-productive" to be helpful in the context of such a hectic lifestyle. If this is the case, we may need some help with the bigger picture of what it means to be connected to God and how essential it is to the kind of life we truly desire. We may also need to sit down and review how we spend our time and ask some tough questions about where we want to be six months or a year from now in terms of our relationship with God.

There are some who simply have trouble believing that conversations with God could really make that much difference. Many of us have experienced the kind of prayer life that does very little to feed our soul. It is easy to run out of motivation when our efforts seem to produce so little fruit. If conversational prayer looks like one more thing we are supposed to do in order to be a good Christian, then we will have difficulty believing that this is anything other than a waste of time that could be better spent doing something else.

What I want to tell you is that if you have never tried the kind of conversational prayer life I am describing here, then this may all sound like a foreign language. Engaging with God and hearing him speak into your life bears very little resemblance to the more traditional forms of prayer that are more like one-way messages from us to God.

A conversational relationship with God is in fact what we were made for. Life is not about doing more than the next person or doing it better or getting far enough ahead to be able to take it easy. For that matter, it is not about "arriving" anywhere. We were designed for relationship with God, first and foremost. *Everything else was meant to flow from the person we become as a result of that relationship.* When we squeeze out God because we have so much to do, we stand life on its head and risk missing it altogether.

I know this may be hard for some people to believe, because many Christians have never experienced a sustained approach to prayer that brings real life. If you have never had this kind of relationship with God, *whatever it is that you have already experienced may seem like all that is possible.* But once you have tasted the goodness of God's voice and experienced his healing words, his personal guidance, and his ever-present love, living without his presence and his voice will feel like going without food and water. We need him more than we know. *Time spent with God is a feast and a foundation for life, not an imposition on our time.*

For those who feel an exceptionally strong need to be productive with their time, I would suggest that you take an extended retreat day (that should really stir up your feelings about it!) and ask God why you feel so compelled to be productive, and see what he has to say about it. The truth is that many of us have learned to be valuable by being indispensable in some way to somebody or to something. We need to hear from God himself why we really matter.

An Alternative

I understand some people truly do have compelling reasons why they have so little time to sit down with a journal. No doubt that was also the case for most people in Jesus' day where an agrarian way of life might have required sixteen hours of work a day just to survive. Such a demanding lifestyle is probably one reason why God instituted the Sabbath, so that one day out of seven his people could rest and turn their mind to the things of God for a sustained period of time.

If you are convinced that your time is completely booked up, I would suggest that you set aside a couple of hours on your day off where you can drink deeply from the well of life and receive the good things that God has for you. Then during the rest of the week, begin each day by taking ten minutes to read over the journal entry from your weekend conversation, and allow the Spirit of God to remind you how much you are loved and what God gave you in your time together. Chewing on one morsel for a week at a time can go a long way toward feeding your soul and strengthening your relationship with God.

More Help With Focusing

One of the beautiful things about conversational prayer is that we can continue to grow in all aspects of it for the rest of our life. Which means there is always more of God, more life, and greater depth for us to experience. Growing in the area of focusing is an important part of that. As we continue to learn how to turn our heart toward God and open up to his presence, our whole being becomes more and more oriented toward life in the Kingdom, and our dependence upon God begins to feel more natural. So whether a person finds it easy to focus their heart on God or whether they often struggle to do so, learning more about entering God's presence is always helpful.

Let's begin here by acknowledging that some people really have a great deal of difficulty calming their mind or focusing on one thing for any length of time. There can be several reasons for this sort of problem, ranging from basically never having learned how to be quiet, to a severe need to stay productive or a need to keep from noticing one's own life. On the lower end of the spectrum, the problems can often be dealt with by taking each anxious thought to God and asking for his healing hand in whatever may be the root causes. At the high end of the continuum, people who cannot quiet may need to seek outside help in addressing the underlying issues that keep their mind in high gear all the time.

In any case, if quieting seems difficult do not despair. Often by focusing on God and experiencing his presence, many of the issues that keep people from quieting can be addressed and healed, paving the way to fewer distractions and better connections with God. In other words, quieting is not an absolute prerequisite to hearing, but rather an aid to hearing *more* and hearing more *clearly*. As we quiet we can hear better, and as we are drawn into the presence of God by hearing and seeing what he wants to show us, we are more able to quiet.

From a purely practical perspective, there are a number of things you can do that will help with this process. To begin with, the time of day you choose can make a big difference in how successful you might be at managing external distractions such as the phone or the needs of your children. A physically calm environment is far more conducive to hearing the promptings of the Spirit than a noisy room with lots of interruptions.

Because of how God has joined together our physical, mental, and spiritual components, and because quieting and focusing are very physical acts as well as mental and emotional, we can often dial down our stress level with such simple things as taking a few deep breaths, yawning, stretching our shoulders and back, and getting adequate sleep the night before. Although these things might not sound very "spiritual," they can be extremely helpful in calming our nervous system and engaging the relational circuits within our brains (Wilder and Khouri).

For most people, music can also help them relax and quiet. In an interesting episode during the history of Israel, there was a gathering of three kings who asked Elisha to talk to God on their behalf (2Kings.3:4-21). But things did not go smoothly and by the time he finally agreed, Elisha was fairly upset. So he asked for someone to come and play the harp for him. While the musician was playing, Elisha had an encounter with God and received a word for the kings. This is a great example of how music can help us to focus better.

I recommend finding at least one or two songs that speak strongly to you, and keeping them handy to help you quiet your soul and enter into your time with God. If you know how to burn a CD, make an entire album of your favorites to listen to whenever you need them.

The book of Psalms is in its entirety a collection of songs and poems that have been used by the Jewish people for centuries to help them remember who they are and what kind of God they are dealing with. Many of those Psalms are still wonderfully effective in bringing us to a place of receptivity and anticipation of God's presence. Something as simple as a phrase from Psalm 84 can be used to usher us into the presence of God.

> "My soul yearns, even faints, for the courts of the LORD;
> my heart and my flesh cry out for the living God" (Ps.84:2).

Building a small collection of these gems can be very useful when you need help with focusing. All it takes is a glance at one or two passages like this, and our heart remembers who we are and whose we are.

Dealing With Distractions

There are other issues to deal with as well. For some people, as soon as they try to quiet, things begin to bubble up in their awareness that have been temporarily forgotten such as bills to pay and errands to run. One way to deal with this kind of intrusion is to keep a separate piece of paper handy on which you can write down whatever comes to mind that you do not want to forget. Letting the paper hold the thought frees you to relax again without worrying about that particular item.

With some kinds of nervous energy, you may on occasion find it difficult to relax at all, especially when feeling angry or excessively anxious. Some people just seem to have an over-abundance of energy that makes them fidgety whenever they try to sit for very long. In these cases, pacing around in a fairly calm area may be more beneficial than trying to sit in one place. While this can present some challenges in terms of recording your time with God, it is preferable to have a qualitatively better connection with him than to be so uncomfortable that your focus suffers.

Remember, too, that some people have a nervous system that is in high gear all the time, and they have learned how to focus their attention in several directions at once while staying connected both relationally and emotionally. If you are truly able to fully engage in this way and you find that trying to quiet is more distracting than helpful, then please feel free to experiment with whatever approach works best for you. The important thing is to be able to focus well enough to reflect on your conversation and listen to the promptings of the Spirit at the same time.

Using the Eyes of Our Heart

Focus actually refers to a *dual process* of taking our eyes off "things on the earth" setting them on "things above" (Col.3:2). These are really two parts of the same process. When it comes to spiritual things, it matters a great deal what fills our vision. That is why Paul tells us to set our eyes on God and what is good.

So while people often find it helpful to empty their mind for a few minutes in order to relax, when our intention is to hear from God we need to beyond emptying and invite him to fill our vision, looking for him with the eyes of our heart.

As you focus your attention on God, it can be very helpful to picture yourself having a conversation with him. You might see yourself sitting on a hillside with Jesus, resting in the arms of your heavenly Father, or even having every cell of your body permeated by Spirit of God.

I realize that some people have concerns about whether or not it is alright to use our imagination to connect with God. There are even some prominent Christian leaders who have spoken out against holding images of God in our mind, usually citing the second commandment and its prohibition in regard to making or worshiping any *physical* images of God. Others fear that forming mental images is somehow New Age, and therefore Christians should avoid using their imagination this way.

If you have no problem in regard to using your imagination in prayer, please feel free to skip to the next segment titled, "A Metaphor of Three Chairs," as the rest of this section is addressed those who have reservations or concerns about how Christians can use their imagination toward spiritual ends.

First of all, while I agree completely that there is such a thing as a misuse of the mind, we need to be careful not to "throw the baby out with the bathwater." If we stop and think about it, turning off our imagination is actually quite difficult, if not impossible. You may have just imagined a baby being poured out with the water from a small tub! Or you may have pictured what it would be like to turn off your imagination with a switch.

The truth is that God deliberately created our minds with the capacity to "see" things that are not in our immediate field of vision. Our imaginative capacity allows us to picture better ways of doing things, it allows us to rehearse possible outcomes before attempting something difficult, and it allows us to transmit meaning with stories and metaphors that are far more potent than descriptive prose can be. That is one of the reasons why Jesus used word pictures all the time in his teaching. Bible stories stir up our imagination and give us a chance to compare our own responses to those of the characters in the text.

For example, it is one thing to be told that God forgives us unconditionally and quite another to hear the parable of the Prodigal Son. The image of a father running out to meet his long-lost son can communicate very powerful meaning that penetrates far deeper than any forensic description of forgiveness. Stories are so important that many times in both the Old and New Testaments we are told to *remember* the things that God has done for us. In that sense we are *commanded* to use our imaginations in a holy way that actually brings us *closer* to reality. This is not at all the same thing as engaging in fantasy which moves us *away* from what is real.

The ability to misuse imagination does not prohibit our use of it any more than our ability to curse should prohibit us from talking. Abandoning our ability to picture holy things would actually make parables incomprehensible, put much of our mind out of reach of God's redemption, and violate the command to love God "with all your mind." How does one think about whatever is "lovely, pure, true, just or commendable" (Phil.4:8) without imagining how those things might look in the real world?

How do you "remember the Lord's death" without seeing him on the cross? How do we "fix our eyes on Jesus" (Heb.12:2) when he is no longer here in the flesh?

We could go on. Story telling has been used from the beginning of time to teach important principles to children so they can learn from the experiences of others without having to make all the mistakes themselves. That is most certainly a use of our mind intended by God.

When we read that the psalmist longed to "behold the beauty of the Lord" (Ps.27:4) what are we supposed to think went through his mind, given that he could never really *see* God? When Jesus told the disciples that the Holy Spirit would become their new teacher, did he not intend for them to think about how those conversations would be both similar to and different from the way Jesus had taught them? When the first generation of disciples broke bread together in remembrance of Christ, did not images of Jesus come to mind? Is it now wrong for us to imagine him breaking bread because we never saw him in the flesh?

This fear of using our imagination really makes very little sense. Consider the value of seeing God's gift to us as a "treasure in earthen vessels" (2Cor.4:7) or envisioning ourselves as clay in the potter's hands (Isa.64:8). Imagination is a good thing, because it helps us know who we are, where we have come from, and who this God is who cares so much about us. It truly is a good thing to imagine ourselves having a conversation with God!

As for the possibility of crossing over to New Age practices, when we begin to fill our mind with thoughts of God and seek to connect with him deeply, we put great distance between us and any cult practice where people try to connect with whatever happens to be flying through the cosmos. All we really need to do is ask God to guard our heart and mind, and trust him to meet us in the process.

The only caution I might add, is that for those who have had extensive experience in the occult in the past this may be a bit more complex. People who have a history of direct contact with demonic forces may need special help sorting things out in their mind and prayer life. Even then, many may be able to simply trust that God will will protect them and expose any pictures in their mind that are from the enemy.

A Metaphor of Three Chairs

At this point I would like to share a particular a set of images (from Wilder and Coursey) that many people find helpful in their efforts to focus well and engage with God.

Imagine a lush green hill. At the top of the hill there are three chairs. Jesus is sitting in the chair on the right which is turned toward the other two chairs. The chair in the middle is facing him and we call that the Direct Interaction chair. The chair on the left is facing away from him and we call that the Appreciation chair.

When it comes to having a conversation with him, there are three main options open to me. The first is to sit at the bottom of the hill, perhaps in a thorn patch that has captured all of my focus and attention, and try my best to pray. I think you can see how this could really make quieting and focusing on God almost impossible. We fill our mind with whatever is troubling us and ruminate on it until we can think of nothing else. At that point it becomes extremely difficult to see Jesus and he seems very far away.

My second option is to sit in the Appreciation chair on top of the hill, facing away from Jesus. I may not be able to see him and I may even have difficulty hearing what he is saying to me. But I know he is near and I can focus my attention on the goodness he has shown me and the goodness of his character, setting my affections on "things above." I may even get a sense of his presence there with me. Spending time in appreciation is incredibly good for my soul, which is why there are so many admonitions in the Bible about being thankful and having a grateful heart. Perhaps even more important, this way of connecting with God can often be a part of finding my way to the next chair.

From the Direct Interaction seat I can see and hear Jesus and engage with him in conversation. He can mentor me, console me, and even heal broken places in my soul as I receive healing and goodness that come from his presence and voice. I can ask him about the thorns at the bottom of the hill as well as other things I do not understand, and engage with him about every aspect of my life.

So whenever I find myself thrashing around in the thorns, wondering where God is and why I cannot see him, remembering this image and asking God to help me find my chair of Appreciation will often lift me out of that place. It especially helps if I have some really strong areas of appreciation that I can bring to mind whenever I need to. Once I begin to feel that appreciation and the growing sense of his presence, I can ask him to help me find the place of Direct Interaction and begin talking with him about what I need.

The presence of God is an awesome thing. Being with God can restore our soul and give us life. If you have never spent much time resting in God's presence, I would encourage you to try taking a few significant time-outs just to learn how to be with him and experience the security of surrendering to him – body, soul, and spirit.

The more we learn to quiet our mind, the more naturally we will be able to engage with him directly and hear his voice. And the more we learn to refocus our heart on mind on God, the easier it will be to quiet.

Lord, I pray that you would help me quiet my heart and mind. Let me see the beauty of Your presence. Help me to receive Your peace into my heart and rest in You. Those times when I need others to help me quiet, I ask that You would lead me to the right people. Help me to believe You are truly good and that You are here to bring life to me. In Jesus' name ...

REFLECTION QUESTIONS

What strategies have you used in everyday life to quiet yourself when you are upset? When you are afraid? How might these practices be useful in your conversations with God?

DISCUSSION QUESTIONS

Do you ever experience God's presence? If so, what is it like? What are the factors leading up to your awareness of his presence? If you have not had much experience of this, what do suppose might help?

EXERCISE 1

Create an Appreciation List to help you quiet and focus.
1. Identify at least six things in your life that you view as gifts and for which you feel a great deal of appreciation. Do not include material items, unless they were basic necessities that were restored.
2. Shorten the list to the three which most easily impact your mood when you think about them.
3. Give each item on the list a short name. For example, if you have a really good memory from when you first began to date your spouse, you could name it your "Dating" memory.
4. Memorize the list.
5. Each morning as you are waking up, rehearse the list in your mind and allow yourself to feel the gratitude that you associate with each item. Do this until you have no hesitation in remembering the list.

At this point you can use this list whenever you want to reconnect with God. Just bring the items to mind and turn your eyes to him.

Exercise 2

This exercise is intended to help you with the Focusing aspect of conversational prayer.

1. Ask God to help you sense his presence with you.
2. Read the passage below.
3. Begin to *seek* the Lord with your heart (this is not a passive exercise). Record any pictures, impressions, emotions or words that come to mind.
4. Spend at least 10 minutes focusing on being with God and holding these thoughts. When your mind begins to drift, do not chastise yourself. Simply notice, smile, and turn your eyes back toward God.

Psalm 27:4,8 (NRSV)

This Psalm was probably composed out in the desert somewhere, with the writer imagining what it would be like to live in the Temple 24/7.

> "One thing I asked of the Lord, that will I seek after;
> to live in the house of the Lord all the days of my life;
> to behold the beauty of the Lord, and to inquire in his
> temple...'Come,' my heart says, 'seek his face!'
> Your face, Lord, do I seek."

After the Exercise

Did you have any sense of the presence of God?
Did you have any reactions you would like to share with others?
Note that connecting with God and enjoying his presence is an important form of prayer in and of itself!

Chapter 6 – Listening

"Listen carefully to me and eat what is good" (Isa.55:2).

Learning how to listen to the gentle promptings of the Spirit is perhaps the most important thing you will ever do. Several bridges have already been described that can help us engage with God in conversation, such as spending time in appreciation, actively reflecting on spiritual things, using Scripture as a starting point for discussions, using our imagination in holy ways, and allowing God to stir our longings for him. In this chapter I want to further expand these areas and say more about how God talks to us. I will also explore some of the various forms our conversations with him can take.

The Holy Spirit as Our Mentor

As we consider how God engages with us in conversation, it is helpful to think in terms of how an ideal mentor might work with an apprentice. If you were to ask your mentor a question like, "What should I do about my unreasonable boss?" you would not expect him or her to give you some compact ready-made solution like *Three Steps to Managing Your Unreasonable Boss in Seven Minutes or Less*. Rather, a good mentor would probably ask you questions about your interactions with your boss, why you describe him as "unreasonable," and what kinds of responses inside you get triggered when you talk to him – things that make interacting with him so difficult. Your mentor may even challenge a few of your underlying assumptions, such as what you think a workplace should be like, or your expectations for fairness and kindness in an imperfect world.

By the time you get to an "Aha!" and a clearer vision of how to proceed, you may no longer be able to identify who said what or how you got to the understanding you needed. All you know is that you spent time with your mentor and came away with something you did not have before you talked things out. Hearing from God is often a similar process.

Knowing that God often interacts with us in this collaborative manner does a lot to free us from trying to look for something more sensational or feeling like we need to be able to quote God. I can begin my conversation with him by writing out my own thoughts and feelings about an issue, move on to asking some questions about it, exploring some of the options, and then suddenly see a glimmer of light that leads me to some insight that I need for my life.

When I'm done, I can summarize what I've learned in a few sentences perhaps, without prefixing any of it with "Thus says the Lord." They may well be all my own words, capturing to my best ability the impressions I received from God regarding the issue at hand. In fact, this is quite literally the form that many of the Psalms take.

As an example of how God mentors us, Jesus was once asked whether or not the people should pay taxes to Caesar (Lk.20:22-25). He could have responded easily enough with a "Yes" or "No." Although they would have received an answer, they would not have learned much. So instead, he engaged the crowd in a discussion about *What Belongs to Whom*, and those who were paying attention and were teachable came away with an appreciation for the claim of God on their lives and a lot less anxiety about funding the coffers of their oppressors.

Jesus' way of approaching the issue went far beyond the crowd's desire to know the "right" answer, even though the question was a valid one. He helped them see their dilemma though the eyes of heaven, which not only pointed them in the right direction as far as their choices were concerned, but gave them a better understanding of how to discern God's heart in the matter. He changed the entire discussion *from a question of ethics* (Is it wrong for a Jew to pay taxes to a pagan ruler?) *to a question of identity and relationship* (Who am I as a Jew and how does my relationship to God impact how I relate to this world?). In so doing, he drew his listeners into a deeper relationship with God and away from their preoccupation about what made them right or wrong.

As an aside, when I wrote those words above about Jesus changing the issue from ethics to identity, I felt a life-giving quality in the words and my heart responded with a resounding "Yes." I believe that was an example of God speaking to me as I wrote. My original intent was merely to demonstrate how God can speak into a situation and help us to see it differently. But as I wrote, an extra dimension came to mind about how deeply he re-framed that event, and that insight felt like a refreshing breath of air.

Of course, not all of our conversations with him will be about mentoring us in Kingdom living. Sometimes he just wants to comfort us, express his love for us, or encourage our heart. These are important and life-giving as well.

Personalized Revelation

Our heavenly Mentor knows exactly what we need and how we need to hear it. So we can expect him to personalize his revelations to us in ways that might not mean much to anyone else. I will give an example here of something that meant a great deal to me but as far as I know has never impacted anyone

I shared it with, because God tailored this message to fit my need and it was not intended for anyone else.

During a conversation with God, I was agonizing over an important relationship in which the other person was a constant reminder to me of someone in my past who had been very toxic and hurtful. Suddenly an image came to mind of a small oval shape with a dot in it toward one end. I knew immediately what it meant. That oval represented who they were in their entirety and the dot represented the part of their personality that resembled the person from my past. God was showing me that I was not seeing the whole person as well as how much relative importance *he* put on that issue in their life. Instantly, this simple picture dramatically altered how I interacted with that person from then on.

Now that image means almost nothing to anyone else, and most everyone who has heard this story has said they do not understand how I knew what it meant or why it made such a difference to me. But for me it was like a revelation, and I knew instantly the problem was not so much the other person as it was my own eyesight. God tailored his response to what I needed to see. The fruit of that revelation was plain enough, which confirmed that the source was God. The point is that this was a very personalized way of helping me see what I needed to see.

I also want to draw attention to the fact that God spoke to me without words. Instead of providing some long explanation of my poor understanding of this person, God gave me a glimpse of how he saw them, using a symbol that I would understand. Once I saw the truth of it, I explored it at length in my journal, including writing out my prayer to God for a change of heart. But that image stuck with me, and it came to mind over and over in the months that followed whenever I talked to this person. It was as if I carried with me a constant reminder of how God saw them, and it profoundly changed my perception and our interactions.

As a side-note on discernment, if I had seen an image in my mind that left me confused, I probably would have asked God if it came from him and what it meant. If that led me nowhere, then I would have most likely dismissed it as a product of my own imagination. When God speaks to us, we can generally tell it is from him by the sheer quality of what we receive and the fruit that it bears.

How We Are Involved In Hearing God

An important thing to understand here is the nature of spiritual revelation and the manner in which God speaks to us. Since he mostly communicates with us Spirit-to-spirit, much of what we receive from him comes to us in the form of impressions and images that we then shape into words so we have something concrete to deal with. In the process, God often makes use of symbols and ways of speaking that we are already familiar with.

He may remind us of old memories or previously memorized Scripture passages. He may bring up metaphors that are personally meaningful to us, or even combine several elements of our prior learning and experience at once and then show us how they apply in our present context.

So while we can refer to the end result as "something we received from God," much of the time it would be inaccurate to say that we are quoting him verbatim. We are virtually always *interpreting* or *paraphrasing* what we receive from him. Even when we hear fairly clear messages, we must understand that most of the time we ourselves are in some way instruments of his communication.

Properly understood, this perspective on how God speaks to us is very freeing and affirming. To begin with, we do not need to be afraid of mixing some of our own thoughts in with what we are hearing from God. We can be quite certain of it! We simply need to maintain an attitude of humility about what we are receiving and remain teachable so that God can continue to refine and renew our understanding as we go along.

As we verbalize the impressions and spontaneous thoughts we have, our own stuff inevitably becomes part of the end result. But that does not necessarily diminish its value. Just as our own imperfect *interpretations of Scripture* can lead us to life-changing truth, so also our best understanding of what God is giving us directly can be life changing. The good news is that even a little light or a little insight can make a huge difference in our life.

Rephrasing this another way, there are two reasons why it is valuable to know that I am an integral part of the process of hearing God. First, it helps me with my discernment, because I am always open to hearing better or knowing more than I do now. It infuses a very healthy dose of humility into my conversations, because I am always learning, always refining my understanding.

Second, I am relieved of the burden of trying to be infallible in my listening process. I hear the best I can and put on paper the best words I can find to capture what I believe God is telling me. That is more than enough to feed my soul and change my life. I can know that all of the life-giving, life-changing stuff came from God without having to pretend I can defend every word on the page as gospel.

Again, once we know this we can for the most part set it aside and proceed with our conversations much the same way that we would any conversation in which we might attempt to paraphrase what we are hearing. If we are paying attention, we generally hear most of what someone says and can even repeat the heart of what they say quite well, without getting every single word exactly the way they delivered it. But that in no way diminishes the value of what they said or our best attempt to restate it. Just because we are involved on the receiving end does not mean that we cannot trust our conversations with God. There is every reason to believe that he is more than able to assist us in getting the substance of whatever he wants us to know.

This does not mean that God will never speak clearly and directly into our mind. He does. And when he does we can rejoice in his gift to us and treasure those words. But that is not the only way he speaks to us, and we need not be disappointed if he chooses the more common approach of impressing a matter on our heart and allowing us to participate by finding the words to flesh it out.

My prayer for you is that as you see how God can enter into your reflections and assist your thinking, you will be able to broaden your expectations for how God can speak into your life.

What Can We Expect in This Process?

Once we get started with reflecting and listening, what can we expect to happen in the process? What sort of things can we expect to receive? Hopefully, answering some of these questions will help you to expand your vision of what conversational prayer might look like.

Expect Spontaneous Thoughts and Images

As stated earlier, when we learn how to hear what God is saying to us and how to be led through our conversations (rather than trying to work out an understanding by reason alone) we will begin to notice thoughts and images coming to mind that we would not have come up with on our own. This seems to be the most common way in which God speaks directly to our heart.

Of course, we are all capable of being spontaneous and having thoughts jump into our head that are not from God. But with experience we can learn to tell the difference between our thoughts and his thoughts, primarily by the fruit they bear, such as the sense of joy and peace that follows his voice. We will discuss this in more detail in the chapter on Discernment.

In the reflection I described earlier where I was thinking about how Jesus emptied himself and came to earth, I initially focused on the godly attributes he must have set aside – like being everywhere at once and not being limited by time. When I began to think about what he still had left after that, the idea of *relationship* jumped into my mind very unexpectedly. One of the things that made that thought very different from my own was that I was trying to identify various *attributes* of God, and *relationship* was not a word I would have used. I had a strong sense it was God's idea due to the fact that it was something outside my own pattern of thought.

Why Not Just Speak Directly To Us?

I used to wonder why God talks to us this way rather than just speak into our inner ear or something like that so we could be sure of what he said. But I'm beginning to think he really does know what he's doing! First, he wants to write his words on my heart (Heb.10:16) not simply say things *to* me. This seems to be particularly true when he is offering an insight into something I did not know before or when he is in the process of reframing an event so that I can see what I have been missing. In this way he often reveals truth to my heart even before I have the words for it, like an intuitive leap that my mind has not quite grasped. As I reach for it mentally, it begins to take shape in words that make sense. And when I finally write it out, the words have the ring of truth to them.

This is especially true when it comes to inner healing. During one of my last big encounters with God regarding my life-long struggle with self-hate, I was struck by the idea that self-hate must be built entirely of lies because it always assaults my God-given identity. In the moment I saw this, I was fairly sure that God had revealed it. At the same time I was hardly able to believe that so much of my identity could be made up of smoke and mirrors, because no one had ever explained it to me that way before. So it took some time to work out in words what I had already received in my heart. But I never forgot it. This was a perfect example of how God can begin writing his truth on our heart even before we can make sense out of it with our mind.

Second, and somewhat related to this, is the idea that what he wants to give me is not so much a verbal statement as it is a light so I can see differently. When God reveals something about how he sees my situation, my neighbor, or whatever, the new perception can take hold of me like a dawning awareness and flood my understanding, with or without words. What I know, I know because his Spirit has revealed it. Putting it into words is mostly my own attempt to capture what I have already seen with the eyes of my heart. The revelation itself is more important than the words used to describe it. So whether he begins with words and images, or whether he begins with an understanding that comes *before* the words does not really matter. Either way, by giving me the task of finding words to describe it, he involves me more fully in the process.

Third, I find mysterious beauty and wonder in the idea that evil is loud and violent in its manner, while a small whisper from God is enough to dispel the darkness and heal our wounds. Evil seeks to overwhelm, intimidate, and escalate until everything in its path is destroyed. But God speaks peace into the void and creates life, or touches a leper and heals his flesh. God uses the most simple of means to overturn the work of the enemy. Speaking quietly is one of those ways.

Fourth, God is speaking with us Spirit to spirit, not person to person. It makes sense that our spirit would hear and see differently than our physical body would. Paul emphasizes this when he says that spiritual things are discerned spiritually and not by human means (1Cor.2:13-14).

Fifth, I think this way of communicating with us very much resembles that of a masterful rabbi. Rather than spoon-feed us everything we need to know, he asks us to speak out what he is showing us as part of our learning process. A great example of this can be seen in the Gospels when Jesus asks his disciples, "Who do you say that I am?" While he had given them plenty of evidence, he wanted them to do the work of putting into words what they were starting to believe about him.

By actively participating in working out his revelations to us, we internalize the learning more deeply. As a by-product, we become far more practiced in spiritual discernment. When you see it, this is actually a very ingenious way of writing his ways on our heart rather than simply pouring more information into our head.

Finally, his way of speaking to us is consistent with his desire to draw us to himself and not overpower us or coerce us in any way. We need to be deliberate about paying attention or we will miss what he wants us to know. Seeking connection with him is part of what we need to do in this relationship.

Expect Physical and Emotional Reactions

Often when reading Scripture in a receptive manner we will experience an emotional or physical response to something we run across in the text. We might feel a twinge of shame or a quick wave of anxiety when we see something that reveals part of our heart that we would rather not see. Or conversely, we may feel a rush of God's love or a longing for more of his presence in our life.

These internal reactions can be important indicators of deeper issues of our heart. When they are negative in nature, we may want to stop and talk to God about them. One time when I read the verse, "to whom much is given, much is required" (Lk.12:48) I felt a huge stab of guilt. I began to confess to God my pitiful record and how poorly I live in proportion to what I have been given. As I was on the verge of beating myself up, I suddenly had the thought that *God loves to give* and there was no way I would ever keep up with him and respond "proportionately." He's just not that stingy. I felt a huge weight of condemnation lift off my soul as well as tremendous gratitude for God's generosity.

Consequently, I felt even more drawn to God. We were then able to talk about what I needed to learn in regard to giving away the life-giving things I receive from him, without having to deal with the crushing weight of failure or trying to make up for what I have not done. God wanted to bring some things to my attention, but he had no intention of destroying me with my poor record.

On the other hand, when our internal reactions are very positive in nature, we would do well to savor those moments and not rush on ahead. Spending time adoring our God, feeling his love, or being filled with gratitude for his work in our life can be very important for strengthening our bond with God and building our trust in his goodness. Either way, listening to our internal reactions and talking to God about them is an important part of engaging with God.

Expect Internal Resistance, Hesitation or Doubt

Given our unfinished state, we can expect from time to time that we will push against what God is doing in our life, resisting things he might want to teach us, and even running away from spending time with him.

For example, in spite of how life-giving it is to spend time with God, there are still days when I feel reluctant to sit down and talk with him. I may be particularly busy or I may feel shut down emotionally and would rather stay that way and not talk to anybody.

I suppose I could force myself to open up my Bible to where I left off the day before and go through the motions of journaling. But what usually works a lot better is to start writing about why I would rather not talk right then. God sometimes shows me things about my attitude that I need to see, or opens my eyes to some relevant truth I need at that particular time. As he reveals my heart and why I am resisting his input into my life, most of the time my desire changes and I begin to long for his touch and his presence.

By acknowledging my resistance and taking it to God, my heart is softened in ways I would probably not experience if I either steamrolled over my negative feelings or gave into them and walked away. That is why when we notice any resistance, it is generally better to take it to God without trying to sanitize it first or fix it on our own. Trying to overpower or suppress our internal resistance will only deprive us of an opportunity to be mentored in our time of need and to grow closer to God.

Expect Better Questions

Spending time with God can have a number of unexpected side effects, such as discovering that we know far less than we thought we did about life in the Kingdom. As we seek to be led in our conversations with God, we may find that our questions need as much help as anything. And looking for better questions to ask is part of the job of an apprentice.

Slowing down to *ask the obvious* is one of the ways our eyes can be opened to valuable insights. A verse like, "O Lord, you have searched me and known me" (Ps.139:1) may yield multiple treasures if we ask things like:

- Does being searched feel like a good thing or a scary thing?
- What does it mean to be known by God?
- What fears, if any, does this elicit in me?
- What comfort can I find in this?

Or when we read in Isaiah 55 that we can buy wine and food without money, is this simply a poetic way of saying "free food!" or is there more to it? Why does he contrast his free banquet with "spending your labor on that which is not bread"?

Instead of assuming we know what some word means, it can be very rewarding to ask God to unpack some of the terms with which we are familiar. For example, what does he mean by "food" and "water"? How do we actually "eat" his words? Or when Jesus says, "*Abide* in me" (Jn.15:4-5) what does that mean? What would "abide" look like? How is that different from just thinking about him once in a while? Seeking to be curious about the ordinary things we encounter in the text or in life can be very revealing.

Another way that better questions can rise to the surface of our awareness is by paying attention to our reactions, as noted above. While trying to help a friend deal with his self-rejection I suggested that he ask God, "Lord, how do *you* see our relationship right now?" But my friend was not sure he wanted to know God's answer to that particular question. So I suggested he slow the process down some and ask, "Lord, what do I need to know about my own heart, about grace, or about you, that would calm my fears about that other question?" My friend said he thought that was something he could do.

So we approached God together with that question and God gave us an amazing insight: *Grace means that God considers the relationship to be more important than our messy life. We do not have to*

earn God's approval in order to have a relationship. He establishes our
relationship first, and that leads to our restoration.

God wanted a relationship with my friend no matter how
battered he saw himself. There was no need to "clean up his act"
so that God would approve of him. Instead, we get the
relationship first, and that forms the context for the work that
needs to be done. For my friend that was great news, and it paved
the way to meeting with God more deeply than he had known
before. By paying attention to the anxiety that the first question
caused in him, we were able to move to a better question that
brought the very light he needed.

Often those better questions come from God himself, helping
us to find what is important. We see this in the ministry of Jesus.
Again, when asked whether to pay taxes to Caesar, he responded
with another question, "Whose picture is on this coin?" That in
turn led to a better answer. It is all part of how a rabbi might lead
his apprentices to new understanding.

When we begin to see ourselves as students of life who are
truly in the earliest stages of discovery and who do not need to
have all the right answers, a whole new way of proceeding opens
up to us as we seek to relearn all there is to know about life from
the one who created it in the first place. There is great beauty in
the simplicity of not knowing or having to think we know more
than we do. Learning to ask obvious and simple questions is very
much a part of that process.

What About Direct Guidance?

There is also another area that needs some clarification. One of
the common ideas about hearing from God is the hope of getting
direct guidance for decisions we need to make. I may want to
know which car to buy so I do not get a lemon, or which job to
take, or whom to marry. We often think of God's will as a specific

set of right and wrong choices that we can make, and want to get a clear direction as to what to do so we make the "right" choice. Any time there is a seminar on how to know the will of God for your life, the place is usually packed out.

While seeking guidance from God is important, this particular concept of finding God's will often gets mixed up with other issues.[7] First, God's will involves much more than choosing "A" or "B." Thinking about God's will only in terms of making good decisions can severely limit the quality of our connection with him. God's overriding will for us is to be in relationship with him no matter what choices we make in everyday matters.

Second, people sometimes seek these kinds of answers as a way of avoiding the work of learning discernment or having responsibility for the outcome. For the most part, making choices is something we need to learn how to do. Third, trying to get the right answer without going through the process of getting there can sidestep the learning that may be available in that situation.

As noted above, Jesus often preferred teaching instead of giving direct answers, choosing to help people see a given situation through the eyes of heaven rather than telling them what to do. If I may use this illustration yet one more time, when asked whether Jews should pay taxes to their oppressor, Jesus could have responded with a simple "Yes." But no one would have learned anything and it would have probably sparked more dissent. Instead he took the opportunity to teach them the difference between what belongs to God and what he leaves to people. This is very typical of how he mentors us in everyday situations.

And yes, there are times when God has something specific in mind and wants us to know what that is. If that is the case, we can

---

[7] David Benner: *Desiring God's Will* is a superb teaching on God's will.

be fairly certain that he will not play a guessing game with us, leaving vague clues around for us to pick up on, but he will let us know what we need to know. And even when we do get that kind of clarity, we might want to consider asking God what else he wants us to know about the issue and seek to become learners in the process.

What Will We Probably Not Hear?

Among other things, it is important to point out that we will *not* hear condemnation. One of the most common barriers to hearing from God is the fear people have that if they open up to him, he will begin to tell them all the things he does not like about them and the things they have been doing wrong. They are afraid that if he can see their heart (which he can) he most certainly must be disgusted with them.

Could this really be what we are in for if he speaks to us? Hear the words of Isaiah to God's people at their absolute worst point of rebellion in their entire history:

> "Listen carefully to me and eat what is good, and delight yourself in abundance. Incline your ear and come to Me. *Listen, that you may live*" (Isa.55:2-3, emphasis added).

Or consider the words of Jesus when he says:

> "Come unto me, all you who are weary and heavy laden, and I will give you rest. Take my yoke upon you and learn of me ... and you shall find rest for your soul" (Mt.11:28-30).

Does this sound like a God who is looking for a way to beat us over the head? Of course he knows our heart. But he also knows there is very little we can do about it and that he is the only one who can repair it. By coming to him you are giving him that opportunity. That is precisely why he speaks *Life* into us and not condemnation. He knows the path to restoration and he loves to give life to his people. Any fear of condemnation we have is based entirely on something other than God.[8]

Of course, you will not receive anything that runs contrary to Scripture. God is not going to reveal to you the date for the apocalypse or give you permission to sell your neighbor's car for extra cash when he's not looking.

But seriously, learning to have conversations with God is not a substitute for studying the Bible. We need the revelation God has given to everyone as a context for our conversations with him, so that we know what kind of God we are dealing with and what his intentions are for us generally. As we learn what things he has made known to all of his people, we can be sure that whatever he reveals to us personally will be in harmony with his general revelation as well. If we are hearing something that runs contrary to his written Word, we need to take it back to God and ask him to help us see where it is coming from.

The Shape of the Conversation

Now that we have a better picture of what God might reveal to us, let's return to an earlier discussion and say more about what the conversation itself might look like.

Two-Way Dialogue

One possibility is that our conversation will take on a sort of back-and-forth style of interaction in which we may ask a question or make an observation, and immediately experience a spontaneous response as though we are having a two-way dialogue with God.

---

[8] "There is therefore now no condemnation for those who are in Christ Jesus" (Rom.8:1).

For example, several places in the book of Ephesians, Paul prays for the Christians in that city. At one point he prays that they "would know his power toward us who believe, the same power he worked in Christ when he raised him from the dead" (Eph.1:19-20). One time after reading that, I began to wonder aloud to the Holy Spirit whether I really knew what Paul was talking about, and it turned into a give-and-take dialogue.

Me: What power? Are you kidding? All I feel today is defeated and hopeless.

HS: But you know what to do. Why are you still trying to run on your own steam when you can see you are crashing?

Me: Because I'm broken, and the world is broken ... nothing is working the way it's supposed to.

HS: Maybe now we are getting someplace.

Me: But praying just doesn't seem to help.

HS: You've hit a logjam, that's all.

Me: I don't want another logjam. I'm tired of logjams. It makes me feel shameful to run into another one.

HS: The only shame is trying to hide a mountain of logs. The mountain is not the problem.

Me: Then tell me what is.

HS: Your resistance about going to the mountain with me and pulling logs.

Me: Don't you hate me because I'm stuck again?

HS: No, that is why I am here. And why I will not let you go.

Me: Don't leave me. I can't take this by myself.

HS: You have my word. It's you I'm concerned about – you keep thinking about leaving.

Me: Yes, I have considered that. But I can't stay here unless you hold on to me.

HS: You have to ask?

Me: I'm sorry. I just feel so hopeless.

HS: Then let's go to the hopelessness.

Me: Lord, I bring to you my hopeless despair. I ask for you to guide me to whatever it is that is buried here. Whatever it takes. I need you desperately.

This way of interacting feels very much like a direct conversation with a mentor regarding a life issue. After a little bantering back and forth, I arrived at the point where I was willing to take my helplessness to God rather than allow it to continue to be a barrier between us. While I do not experience this form very often, in this case it was the process I needed to move my heart and seek him for help.

Teaching Mode

Sometimes the insights we receive are much bigger than a single idea or phrase. A new awareness can have any number of implications that connect to multiple themes in our life, and we may need to explore those areas in some depth so that the original insight can have its full impact.

When this happens we may find ourselves writing down thought after thought in a fashion that feels like we are being taught something we have never studied before. We could also characterize this form of conversation as a spiritual reflection in which most of the material is received rather than drawn from our prior knowledge.

An example of this style can be seen in the Chapter Two reflection titled, "Looking to Jesus" where God taught me more about the nature of joy. I began by asking some questions about what kind of joy could have been strong enough to encourage Jesus as he contemplated what he was going to have to endure. Although I had heard teaching about the cross all my life, God helped me to see several new elements about this event that I had never seen clearly before. In the process he taught me more about where joy comes from and how it can sustain me.

Given that the Holy Spirit loves to teach, we can expect to be taught like this from time to time. As we learn how to listen, we can look forward to these experiences, as they strengthen our faith and help us to see spiritual realities in new ways.

God's Encouragement

As with the teaching mode, this style of communication is experienced primarily as a monologue, delivered to us by God. What makes this different is that its purpose is not so much to convey the truth about some issue as it is to experience God in the moment and how he loves us and will care for us. What we hear may sound like a love letter, an admonition, or an assurance of his presence with us. It may be laced with scriptural phrases or sound very much like a psalm. Here is an example:

A dear woman I know was already feeling very sad and overwhelmed one day when she looked in the mirror and saw a rather large, angry pimple emerging on her face. It was too much. She began to tell God how upset she was about life and that she felt like one big zit. Instantly God spoke to her and told her she was a jewel in his eyes and that he loved her. His encouragement was exactly what she needed. Her heart melted and her soul was reassured of her Father's love.

This form of conversation is very reassuring and uplifting to our soul. We need to hear God's heart for us far more than we know, as we easily doubt his love for us and his presence with us. The more we see ourselves as his children, the more it makes sense that he would speak to us as a good Father would to his child. Being assured of his love and presence and provision is essential to our well-being.

Summary

God speaks to us in many ways. As we open our heart to him and allow him to guide our time together, we may experience any or all of these ways of relating to him. And because he is so creative, he will find other ways of speaking to us as well – through nature, life experiences, or other people.

For those who are learning to hear God's voice, one of the most helpful ways to connect with him is through Scripture. And for that we turn to a spiritual practice that has helped people for centuries.

Lectio Divina

One of the most fruitful ways of engaging with God that Christians have practiced for the last two thousand years is to begin with the words of Scripture.

There are several excellent approaches to Bible study that can greatly benefit any student of the Word.[9] But there is one particular approach to reading the Bible that I would like to emphasize here. It has been used for centuries to engage with God and receive life from the Word. This practice is often referred to by its Latin name, *Lectio Divina* (pronounced LEK-tsee-oh de-VEEN-ah) which translates to "Holy Reading" or "Divine Reading." In ordinary language it means allowing the Holy Spirit to open our eyes and heart to the wondrous things he would have us see in the words of the Bible, things we would never see on our own.

Lectio Divina differs from common Bible study methods in several respects. The biggest difference is that in *Lectio Divina* we ask the Spirit of God to teach us the Word, rather than work

---

[9] I highly recommend: Fee and Stuart.

through a particular method of study. This is not a trivial distinction. Traditional Bible study relies heavily on our powers of reason and reading comprehension to analyze the text and figure out such things as the author's original intent, the context in which the passage was written, what principles might be behind the text, and how we might apply those principles to our life. This is all good for us, and we can benefit greatly from studying the Word in this way.

In contrast, *Lectio Divina* lays the text before God and asks him to be our teacher. We ask God what he wants us to pay attention to, how he wants us to approach it, and where he wants to go with it. Sometimes he digs into the text to show us things we have not seen before, making it come alive with a richness we would have missed had we studied it on our own. Most of the time he will use the text to speak into our life and provide direction, healing, encouragement, or correction. On occasion he will use the text as a springboard for another discussion that is not even directly related to the original meaning of the text.

Of course, our encounter with God through the text can be informed by many of the things we know from traditional methods of study, but those elements are not the primary focus. Rather, our knowledge of the passage simply becomes one more thing we lay before God as we ask him to show us what is important for us at this point in our journey.

Lectio Divina also usually involves going considerably deeper into a much smaller segment of the text than we would normally address in a Bible study. Our entire conversation with God may be focused on a single word or phrase that has captured our attention. Working through a single chapter one phrase at a time like this might take days or weeks, depending on how many ways we feel led to pursue the thoughts that are brought to light by the Holy Spirit. Depth is far more important here than breadth.

How to Read the Bible in the Style of *Lectio Divina*

Over the many centuries that people have used this approach to engage with God, a pattern has emerged that many have found helpful in guiding this process. I would encourage you to consider the following steps and practice them carefully until this becomes a familiar place for you.

1. Ask God to open your heart to whatever he has for you.

2. Select a fairly short passage to read. When possible, pick up where you left off in your previous journal entry. If you are looking for a place to start, please see the suggestions in the Addendum. Limit how much you will consider at one time. Try reading just a few verses or until you see a transition in the text or a change of idea.

3. Read the passage slowly, several times. If something catches your attention, move on to the next step. Otherwise, ask God to draw you to something as you read the passage again. If after several times you are still not drawn to something, consider going on to the next few verses. Keep seeking until something emerges that you feel led to talk about.

4. Write down the reference and the words that you have been drawn to. Start writing what is on your heart, why you feel drawn to these words, what they mean to you, and what gets stirred up in you when you read them.

5. Continue writing as you invite the Spirit of God to open the text and unpack specific words, to show you what matters, how it relates to what is in your own soul, and so on. Everything that was said previously relating to conversations with God applies here.

6. If you start to run out of steam but feel as if there is more to receive, reread the passage again or reread what you have written, being sensitive to whatever new thoughts may come to mind so that you can resume writing.

7. When it seems as if you have reached a stopping point, ask God how you can best carry with you what you have received. He may lead you into a time of thanksgiving, a prayer of repentance, a healing of a previous wound, or any number of things. You may also want to memorize a verse or write something down on a paper and post it where you can be reminded of what God is teaching you.

8. Thank God for your time together.

When looking for a place to start, I would suggest that you *not* try to read through the entire Bible or pick a book like Numbers. Choose something that is rich in terms of its descriptions of our identity or God's character or what he has done for his people, like the passages listed in the Addendum. Break longer segments into bite-size pieces and take time to savor them one phrase per session. Resist the temptation to try and cover a lot of territory.

As you begin your time with God, reading your previous entry can help to create a context for your conversation and even help you open your heart to be more receptive. If you read a few verses and they do not seem to strike a chord, try reading them again a few more times, asking God if there is anything there he wants you to see. Understand that you are not looking to be blown away here. A simple small shift in your attention may be reason enough to stop and look deeper. Above all, take your time.

Please do not underestimate how valuable this can be. If you have never used an approach like this to engage with God and his Word, it may be hard to believe that *this practice is one of the single most important things you can do for your spiritual life.* Engaging with God is always life-giving. To engage with him over his Word can be absolutely incredible. If you try this for a while and it does not bear much fruit, find someone who has some experience with it and ask for help.

Rest assured that God loves to speak to us and teach us about life in the Kingdom. When he opens the Scriptures to us they will come alive in ways that we could never experience through methodical study alone.

Lord, thank You for making Your home with us and for becoming our Mentor for life. Open our eyes to see and our ears to hear what You have for us. Teach us at the "soul-ular" level of our being, beyond our normal abilities to comprehend. Lay our heart bare and reveal Your heart for us as we seek to know what You have for us each time we come to You. Thank You for life. In Jesus' name ...

PERSONAL REFLECTION

Have you ever burned out on Bible reading?
If so, how does that affect your willingness to try a *Lectio Divina* approach to the Scriptures?

What if you could be taught by God himself as you read?

DISCUSSION QUESTIONS

If anyone in your group has experience with a prayer journal, see if they have any entries that they would be willing to share with the rest of the group.

Discuss your experiences of being moved by God and hearing his voice. Try to describe as best as you can what it is like to know what God is showing you even when you do not "hear" the exact words.

EXERCISE

For many people, Psalm 139 has been a source of condemnation and shame. They are fearful that being searched by God will cause them to feel exposed or ashamed of who they are. But that is only because this Psalm has been misread through the lens of performance-based religion.

In truth, this psalmist is ecstatic about God's presence with him and God's knowledge of him (see v.6). Once we see this truth, the psalm becomes a wonderful source of life, because *it describes one of the most fundamental longings of the human heart — to be fully known and loved by a good person.*

For the purpose of this exercise, limit your range to verses 1-5.

1. Re-read the eight steps under "How to Read the Bible in the Style of *Lectio Divina.*"

2. Ask God to open your heart to this psalm.

3. Begin reading the passage slowly. When you feel your soul awakened by some word or phrase, stop and let it sink in.

4. Write down your thoughts, impressions, images, and so on. Proceed with a *Lectio Divina* style of interaction with God.

5. Spend at least 20 minutes reflecting and writing.

After the exercise, share your experience with others. You can talk about what you received from your time of reflection with God, or you can talk about the process itself and what it was like to ask God to open the Scriptures to you. Notice how God tailors his interaction with each person.

Chapter 7 – Discerning

"The sheep follow him because they know his voice. They will
not follow a stranger ... because they do not know the voice of
strangers" (Jn.10:4-5).

Many of us would love to have a complete list of rules to go by to
help us tell the difference between what is from God and what is
not. But apart from a few broad principles, that does not seem to
be what God had in mind for us. By all appearances, he much
prefers that we learn how to engage with him not only for the life-
giving things that he wants to give us, but also for the discernment
to know what is from him.

While that may sound like something of a circular process, it is
absolutely necessary to developing a relationship with him and
trusting *him* to keep us safe rather than trusting our principles.

It is with that in mind, and the knowledge that our
discernment can continue to grow and develop throughout our
life, that we will look at this area a little closer.

DISCERNING THE PROCESS

The best news about discernment is that it is not an entirely new
skill for us to learn. We practice certain elements of it all the time
in our conversations with other people.

Whenever I talk to another person about something that has
real substance (assuming I am focused and emotionally present)
I quite naturally listen and respond to that person on multiple

levels at the same time. I am at once forming a thought, saying what I am thinking, trying to make sense of the discussion, reacting to what the other person is saying and the way they say it, taking notice of my own reactions, and so on. When we slow it down and look at the component parts, the process of having a discussion involves a lot of bits and pieces. But we do most of this more or less automatically due to the fact that we have had thousands of conversations in the past.

Similarly, if we list all the ways we can exercise discernment during our conversations with God, it looks like a lot to consider. So bear in mind that in actual practice most of the things we are going to talk about will present themselves quite plainly, as long as we pay attention to the process. For example, when my mind starts to drift, ordinarily within a few seconds or minutes I will notice that I have started to wander and take steps to refocus. I do not need to go over a checklist every five minutes to see if some discernment is called for. This is really not so different from talking with a friend.

Discerning Our Internal Reactions

Part of what we want to do with this kind of prayer is allow the Spirit of God to reveal the secrets of our own heart and the areas where we need his perspective. To do that we not only have to pay attention to our internal reactions, we also have to be truly honest about the reactions we actually have, rather than worry about sanitizing our conversations or trying to impress God with how much we know.

For example, if I read a verse about the Father giving us whatever we ask for and in the back of my mind I think, "I'm not so sure about that!" then I need to take notice of my reaction and talk to God about my thoughts and feelings. If instead I try to pretend I believe what the verse says when deep in my soul I do not, I miss an opportunity to allow the Spirit of God to probe more deeply into my heart and speak to me about my trust issues.

Sometimes God's word to us feels like turning on a light in a dark room so that we can see what we have not seen before. While attending seminary, I once received a score of 75% on a book review and I was completely devastated. As I was ranting to God about how horrible I was and how everyone else was smarter than me and why I should quit school, a light suddenly turned on. "Wow! That was quite a reaction over one small paper! Seems like I need a lot of affirmation in order to be OK."

It was a part of my heart that I was not aware of until it got challenged. When I took the problem to God, he turned on the light and I could see how tied in I was to getting approval from others. As I began to dig deeper and engage with God for some healing about my own sense of worth, he revealed to me how I had a long history of looking to pastors and teachers for affirmation.

The key element here was noticing how much an external event was rocking my internal world, and taking that observation to God. Then within the conversation itself I continued to pay attention to whatever elements brought me closer to the true meaning of those reactions. In the end, God revealed to me the root cause of the issue, calmed my soul, and healed a part of me that needed reassurance all the time from highly respected people.

Dealing with Pauses in Our Conversation

Chapter Three talked about conversational prayer being a very active process and not a passive one. We do not simply sit with pen ready and wait for God to begin writing with our hand or giving us dictation. We are not mere conduits of his words to us.

In order to have fruitful conversations with God, we need to be actively engaged, deliberately and consciously. In many of the

Psalms, the writer begins by pouring out his heart to God, giving details of life events that matter to him, both good and bad. The thoughts may be rooted in gratitude or anger, trust or fear, wonder or disappointment. But they are all real-time expressions of where the writer was at the moment.

Much of the time, we then see a shift in the style of the writer as he begins to see things more from God's perspective or considers what he has left out. In some cases we even hear God respond to the writer with very specific thoughts and words about what he has said. But all throughout this process, the writer is very much engaged and involved.

At the same time, there are some really good reasons why we might want to take a breather as we talk with God. If we feel a rush of gratitude, love, joy or something similar, we can do our soul a great favor by taking the time to let those feelings wash over us, to bask in them and let them penetrate deeply. Enjoying God and his love for us is a wonderful gift that we honor by holding it for a while and appreciating its value. This is probably what the psalmists are doing when we see the word *Selah* in the text.

When your time with God has been particularly intense, spending a few minutes in quiet before moving on to the rest of your day helps to solidify your experience and gives you a chance to enjoy the calm. Sometimes we simply need to rest in his arms and feel the security of belonging to him.

On the other hand, some pauses need our attention. Sooner or later there will be moments in our conversations when we just seem to draw a blank. Nothing else comes to mind, but we do not feel as if we are done. What do we do with these pauses?

In most cases, we can simply notice that the flow of thoughts has stopped and go back to an earlier point in the conversation to pick things up again. If we are working with a particular verse of Scripture, sometimes rereading the text will stimulate our thinking.

Otherwise, rereading what we have written so far can often trigger another thought or something about which we would like to probe a little deeper.

Simply being curious and asking a lot of questions can go a long way toward restoring our flow of thoughts. Even questions that we think we are supposed to know the answers to can yield unexpected fruit. For example, when Jesus tells the woman at the well, "whoever drinks of the water that I will give them will never be thirsty," I might want to stop and ask myself, "Do I know what he is talking about? Am I thirsty? Have I ever felt so satisfied by the Spirit of God that I did not feel thirsty?" When the woman asks for that water, I might ask myself where or not I still ask for it. And if I am not asking, is it because I think I already have all that I can receive, or because I no longer believe he will give me what I need to satisfy my thirst, or for some other reason? The more ways we can look at something, the more likely it will reveal some treasures.

Another way to get restarted is to ask open-ended questions like, "Is there anything else you want me to know about this?" or "What am I missing?" Also bear in mind that not everything God wants to reveal to us can be reduced to words. He may want us to know that he is with us, that he cares about us, that he is sufficient for our needs, and so on. These are truths that we may receive more experientially than verbally.

Finally, if our conversation seems to be winding down, or if we have simply run out of the time we have, we may want to write down any thoughts "to be continued ..." so we can pick up on those issues again at another time.

Discerning Blocks in our Connection

Sometimes the dead space in hearing from God is not just a pause but a significant block or barrier in connecting with God or perceiving his presence with us. This issue will be addressed in some detail in Chapter Nine. But for now, just be aware that there can be any number of things within us that can get in the way of hearing well. For example, if I am angry at God for not preventing some tragic event in my life, I may have difficulty letting down my guard and trusting him enough to listen. Similarly, if I am afraid of what he might say to me, it will be very hard to open myself up to his Spirit.

When we discern that there is a barrier between us and God, the best thing to do, paradoxically, is take it to God and ask him what we need to know about it. Surprisingly, at times when it is difficult to hear what God has to say about a passage of Scripture, we may still be able to hear him regarding the barrier in our connection. Our attention is being affected by the barrier already, so we may connect better by focusing on the barrier itself.

If talking to God about the barrier proves to be unfruitful, it is best to seek out someone who has experience in helping people connect with God and ask for help. Our relationship with God is our most valuable gift. Whenever something gets in the way, we need to pursue reconnection with him as if our life depended on it.

Summary

By their very nature, conversations with God are somewhat unpredictable. We see this characteristic quite often in the New Testament accounts of discussions with Jesus that went to unforeseen places. There will be times when we need to initiate a conversation or ask a question, and times when we need to follow the leading of the Spirit to see what God wants to talk about. The key is to be always the learner, never the master of this process. Staying curious and always paying attention to the Spirit of God as well as our own internal reactions will serve us well.

DISCERNING THE CONTENT

In any human communication, we want to be able to make sense of the information, to judge its reliability and to be sure we really understand what the other person is saying. When talking with God, making sure we understand what we hear is particularly important. So let's explore this area in more detail and see if we can shed some additional light on what it means to discern the stuff going through our mind.

Our Observations

In writing down our own thoughts and observations, we need to discern as much as possible between those things that *feel* true and those things that are *actually* true. For example, a woman sitting in an oncologist's office may feel terribly alone as the doctor gives her the news that she has cancer. Her perception that God is nowhere around may *feel* true, but it does not reflect the reality that God is with her.

If I read where Paul says "my God will supply all your needs" (Phil.4:19), I may very well see the phrase "your needs" and feel like he is talking to someone else about *their* needs. I eliminate myself from consideration because I assume that my needs will never get met. It is almost as if somewhere between the page and my conscious mind the text gets intercepted by my internal view of life, and it seems normal to me that I am not included in what Paul is talking about. Yet what seems true to me may be desperately in need of God's healing.

When it comes to making observations of our life or of the Biblical text, we need to bear in mind that we all have the ability to significantly filter our perceptions due to our own preconceived ideas, and therefore our observations can be incomplete or even distorted. So from time to time we may have to question our observations to make sure they are accurate. For our discernment to be effective, then, would mean that we notice when we are reacting in ways that we probably should talk to God about so that he can help us separate what is real from what we believe is real.

Our Interpretations of Our Observations

We are continually trying to make sense of what we see and hear, both consciously and subconsciously. When we identify those interpretations with concrete words, it is important for us to be aware that no matter how true our interpretations might feel, they may very well be an incomplete or inaccurate understanding of the situation and in need of God's perspective.

So when I reflect on an unpleasant comment my brother made, I may feel insulted or even violated, or think he owes me an apology, or any number of other things arising from my analysis of that particular interaction. But if I ask God what he sees from his vantage point, I might discover something that makes sense of my brother's behavior, or perhaps receive from God some reassurance that my brother does not get to define who I am. God's way of understanding the bigger picture may be radically different from my own.

That is why one of the best questions we can ask God is, "What am I missing here? What else can you show me about this?" Because no matter how certain we are about our conclusions, there is almost always more that God can reveal to us that we have not yet grasped.

Faulty Patterns that Drive Our Life

Noticing the things we have come to believe about life is a critical step in healing our wounded soul. For example, a person may read in Romans 8 that there is no condemnation in Christ, but still feel like God is condemning them all the time for what they are doing wrong. The condemnation *feels* true, despite what the text says. Getting this out in the open where we can talk about it with God is extremely important.

Proper discernment would tell this person that some kind of disconnect exists between their experience and what they can see in the Bible. Even though they may not be able to see *how* at the moment, they can still acknowledge that it might be possible to receive healing and freedom at some point so that they no longer feel condemned. Noticing this sort of disconnect is often the first step toward their inner healing.

Summary

This short list of things to discern is by no means exhaustive. The point is that every thought can be weighed, and discerning the nature of what is going through our mind helps us ask better questions and to participate better with our Mentor and what he might want to show us.

Where Do Spontaneous Thoughts Come From?

In addition to thoughts that we can clearly identify as our own, in conversations with God we want to be sure to take notice of the things he reveals to us. As we open up to his mentoring, we will often have spontaneous thoughts that come to us without much effort on our part, as if they have been handed to us fully formed. This is often how God speaks to us.

At the same time, we know that we are all capable of having spontaneous thoughts of our own. And this is where some of the more important aspects of discernment come into focus, because the two biggest concerns that people generally have when they first consider having a two-way conversation with God are:

• How to discern what is God and what is not.

• The fear of opening up to something evil.

Of course no one should ever create an opening for evil. And getting confused about whether or not something is from God can be serious, so these are not trivial issues. But we must also be aware that we can become completely incapacitated and hear nothing at all as a result of our own fear.

Ironically, being overly fearful of error actually makes a person *more* vulnerable to the devices of the enemy. Our relationship with God is one that is based on trusting his character more than our own vigilance. The goal then is to find a way to allow the Spirit of God to speak to us, ensure that the enemy cannot use this opportunity to injure our soul, and over time develop a life of conversational prayer that is filled with joy and not fear.

Addressing and overcoming these fears is absolutely essential to our spiritual life. For if we decide to err on the side of *not hearing anything*, then the enemy has already won. In our attempt to avoid him, we have actually withdrawn from our best resource, the voice of God. Instead, we must engage with God for his guidance and learn to navigate these waters so we can continue to deepen our relationship with him.

God, Self, or Satan

We really have only three possible sources for spontaneous thoughts, each with its own characteristics which necessarily influence the quality or nature of the thought. As we learn to recognize these characteristics, our discernment will improve.

When God speaks, the message is consistent with Scripture and with his own character. His voice carries the power of life within it and contains Truth that sheds light on whatever it is that he is addressing. Very often the words feel "clean" or as if they are purging the very darkness from our soul. There is a ring of truth to them, a clarity of meaning and gracefulness in the way they land on our heart and mind.

When Satan plants a thought in our mind, its impact is far different.[10] In its more blatant forms his voice breathes death, hate, violence, despair, or some other vile characteristic. His thoughts will often attack God's character or our identity in Christ very directly. Even in its more subtle forms it divides, accuses, or condemns. His words are almost always contemptuous of someone, somewhere. At the very least they will appeal to our baser instincts.

Even when he attempts to appear as an "angel of light" (2Cor.11:14) he is really not that good at it. (When Paul made that reference, he was in the middle of explaining how with minimal discernment, one could see substantial differences between the ministry of Paul and that of his detractors). The more time we spend with God, the more the enemy's attempts to distract us will become obvious.

In contrast to either thoughts from God or Satan, our own spontaneous thoughts are far less definable and cover a broad range of possibilities. First, we can simply recall thoughts we have had before, bringing them into the current context. Since the previous thoughts could have originated from God, Satan, self, or others, we are back to square one in discerning their real source.

Second, God has given human beings the capacity for inductive reasoning, which means we are quite capable of making an intuitive leap on our own and coming up with a hypothesis about why things are the way they are. While there is no guarantee that our guesses are correct, they may appear to be true unless they are later disproven. This ability can be very helpful when

---

[10] "There is no truth in him. Whenever he speaks a lie, he speaks from his own nature, for he is a liar and the father of lies" (Jn.8:44).

analyzing new objects or when trying to make sense of an experience, but can also cause a great deal of distress if our ideas are faulty.

In any case, at the point where we make an intuitive leap we may experience the idea as a spontaneous thought that seems true to us. If we do not recognize it as our own thought, we could easily think that it came from God, especially if it appears to make sense of whatever we are considering at the time. However, as long as we stay teachable and are willing to ask God how to understand the things we have written down, this kind of thought should not present any real problems.

Let's say, for example, that I am seeking God for some healing because I constantly beat myself up over the most minor mistakes. During my reflection I begin to remember various times when my mother yelled at me and told me how little "common sense" I had. As I consider the impact of those experiences, I can see how there is a part of me that really believes what she said is true, and that is why I am so hard on myself. Then in a flash of insight, I realize her words were not really about me! After all, "the mouth speaks from that which fills the heart" (Lk.6:45). This new idea hits me like a breath of fresh air. The reason my mother said those terrible things was because there was something wrong with *her*! It had nothing to do with me or who I am.

This feels true, and may give me a great sense of relief. It looks like God has shown me the true source of my pain. But if I stop there, I may internalize a belief that is half truth and half lie. Although there is some validity to the fact that the things she said to me reflected more about her own issues than they did about my identity, my heart may have been further deceived in terms of who my mother was. I am still not seeing her the way God sees her, and I could end up being filled with hate and rage unless I keep going and ask God to heal my image of my mother as well.

This mixing of truth and error is not uncommon, because we are flawed recipients of the truth that God speaks into our heart. Again I want to emphasize that this is not a reason to be afraid of what we might hear. It just means that no matter what intuitive leaps we might make or how good they might feel, we must be willing to lay them before God to see if we have put all the pieces together the way he meant for us to receive them. It is generally a good idea to revisit an insight like this within a few days and ask God if he wants to show us anything else about the issue.

Last, spontaneous thoughts can be the result of deeply internalized beliefs rising to the surface of our awareness. For example, suppose while reading Psalm 63 I see the words, "My flesh faints for you, as in a dry and weary land where there is no water" and right away I have a very strong sense of desperate deprivation, accompanied by a fairly clear image in my mind of being perpetually thirsty and begging God for relief. After reflecting on this for a few moments I realize that part of me is quite resentful about God being so stingy with the water I need.

While that thought may feel very true, it is not what the psalmist meant for me to take away from the verse, nor is it a revelation from God about how life works in the Kingdom. If I have learned to be sensitive to the Spirit of God and how to lean on him for discernment, this would probably catch my attention as something deep inside my heart that needs to be brought out into the light, with the goal of healing my own beliefs. The truth is that God is *not* stingy and there are other reasons why I have internalized this belief, reasons he and I need to talk about.

Discerning where thoughts are coming from, then, is largely a matter of noticing their inherent quality. The more life-giving they are, the more likely it is that they originated with God (even if they are something we remember from before). Mundane thoughts are most likely our own. Strongly negative thoughts usually come from our past experiences and often provide great opportunities for healing.

Improving Our Discernment

Developing good discernment takes time and practice. There are also a few important things to keep in mind that will help us grow in this area.

First, this task of discernment is truly a matter for the *spiritual community* to take seriously. Since most of us have been steeped in an individualistic culture this may be a difficult step for us. But we really do need the help of other Christians in order to learn how to discern the voice of God. And often this is our best protection against weird things like, "Go sit on your roof and wait for the rapture." When the Body of Christ commits to learning how to discern, we create a context in which it is safe to practice listening for God and to be mentored by those whose lives reveal that they know what it means to hear from him.

Of course, there is also such a thing as an unsafe group where no one is allowed to exercise discernment except a certain few, or where group-think has become such a problem that anyone who has an independent thought is considered a threat or is ostracized. In such a case it is vital that we see what is going on and get as far away as possible. There must be a balance between the integrity of the community and the maturity of the individual members in order for us to learn good discernment.

Second, God truly honors our efforts to seek him and will help us in this process. Most people who have a clear encounter with God recognize immediately that he is the source, because nothing else has that much life in it. For those whose experience is less clear, we can trust that when we ask God to make a sacred space for listening to him, he will indeed honor that request and will help us discern the thoughts that go through our mind.

This does not mean we will not encounter any resistance or difficulty. If the enemy hates anything, it is when people really start connecting with God. So we should not be surprised if we have trouble with conversational prayer. But neither should we let this interference have the last word. If we continue to seek God's heart, he will reveal himself to us and help us to hear his voice.

Third, we can ask God to help us with our discernment. As we have noted elsewhere, this is somewhat circular in nature (asking God to help us know what he is revealing to us), and yet there are good reasons to ask him. For instance, even when we have a general sense of what God is saying to us, we can still have thoughts of our own mixed in with what God wants us to know. In those cases, God can help us clarify what part is him and what is not.

The example given earlier demonstrates this quite well. Turning my self-hate into hatred of my mother and blaming her for my difficulties was a spontaneous change of mind. But it was in fact a distortion of what God had been trying to tell me. My own view of her got dragged into what was otherwise a genuine healing about being very different from the person she said I was. I correctly discerned that the message regarding my true identity came from God. But I had to ask God to help me be sure about the rest, and that was when I realized my new conclusions regarding my mother were not from God. By going back over the thoughts that came out of my earlier conversation, God helped me discern what part was from him and what part was not.

Still, there will be times when we ask for discernment and get no clarity at all. That in itself is a fairly good indication that we are not hearing very well at the moment and ought to hold the previous thought rather loosely. It may be best to make a few notes about where we are in the process and return to it at a later time or ask a trusted friend to help us.

More About Censorship vs. Discernment

As stated earlier, the fear of hearing wrongly is sufficient by itself to prevent us from receiving much from God. Fear can also keep us from hearing the hidden thoughts of our mind that would be better brought to the surface where they could be exposed to the light. If we are afraid that we might harbor beliefs or attitudes that run contrary to God's best for us, we can actually keep ourselves from seeing what needs to be healed.

For example, if I read in the Word that God knows my heart, I might feel a brief twinge of fear or shame and move on, when it might be better to honestly say to God, "I wish I could hide some of that stuff from you because I am afraid you won't like what you see there." Once I get that out on the table, I can talk to God about why I feel that way and ask him to help me see myself the way he sees me.

Stopping a thought because it is not a "proper" response is a kind of self censorship that can keep us from having a teachable moment. Suppose we read that sin shall no longer have dominion over us (Rom.6:14) and our first reaction is, "I have no idea what he means by that! I can think of several places in my life where it seems like sin has complete dominion." Then we need to honestly own that thought and ask some hard questions of God and our own heart. If we are afraid of exposing something in us that we would rather not see, then we will repress those thoughts until we can no longer hear them. At that point we are no longer open to healing that area.

To put this all another way, running an internal censor is directly counter to making good observations. It is actually the opposite of good discernment. Even though we may have good intentions in being so vigilant, the real result is that our fear gets in the way of self honesty and keeps us from seeing what God wants to do with our heart.

Fear of Hearing the Wrong Things

Christians sometimes harbor a great fear of hearing something from the enemy. The true antidote for this fear is trusting God, instead of trying to censor our thoughts. When we set aside time to listen for God's Spirit to speak to us, we really can trust God to protect our time with him such that we will not be "taken over" by anything evil. In opening up to God, we are not opening up to whatever is in the vicinity, spiritually speaking. We can be sure that God will protect our soul from an invasion against our will.

That does not mean that we cannot have thoughts that are misleading or even evil, which is why we need to learn to discern what is true from what is not. But we do not need to be *afraid* of those thoughts. We are learners, not masters. The Kingdom of God is about *growing* in grace and discernment, not about *being perfect*. Grace truly covers the deepest thoughts that come from our flesh as well as any lies we might hear from the enemy.

As we present our thoughts to God, he will reveal what we need to know about them. If we are harboring thought patterns that need to be changed, he will work with us without condemnation to bring about the transformation we need. If the thoughts seem like insights but sound a bit odd, he will help us tell the difference between what came from him and what did not. Trust is the key issue here. We *can* trust that (1) God will show us what is true, and (2) that God really is alright with our attempts to learn how to hear from him, however imperfect we may be.

Discernment is not about *preventing* faulty ideas from forming in our minds, it is about *noticing* the thoughts that *do* form and making a *decision* about what to do with what we have observed. We simply need to remain teachable, open to changing any assumptions we make along the way, and trust that God is able to show us what we need to see. He is big enough to help us when we get things mixed up, and he has been doing this a long time.

Quite often I write a thought down in my prayer journal and then immediately have a negative reaction to what I have written. Something about the tenor of the statement does not sound right. Having noticed my reaction to the thought, I then ask God what I need to know about that, and what usually follows is some form of clarification or a rephrasing of the statement so that it better reflects what I need to hear. The point is to remain teachable, depending on God for my security.

What we need to see is that the fear of receiving something bad will not protect us in any case. It is a waste of energy and is rooted in the faulty belief that we could actually catch all the tricks our mind can play on us and all the lies the enemy can say to us. We simply are not up to it, and God does not expect us to do his job. It is better to accept the truth, that we are learners and we will always be learners. Getting it all perfect is not the goal here.

Discernment must always be rooted in our trust of God's grace. Every good gift from God is an opportunity to grow closer to him and receive his word deep into our heart. Every doubting or faulty thought is an *invitation* to pursue more dependence and renewal. Either way, we win!

Bear in mind, too, that in hearing from God the goal is to engage with him and receive life from the conversation, not to come away with infallible quotes like "God said thus and so." Receiving clear messages is wonderful when it happens. But we do not have to have a quoted statement in order to know that God spoke to us about something.

The Value of Experience

Nothing is as valuable as first hand experience to teach us how to discern God's voice. As we seek to engage him and see the evidence in the fruit that it bears, we will learn what connecting with him feels like and sounds like. We gain familiarity with the heart of God and learn to discern his voice by the life that is evident in the things he reveals to us.

Over time, this experience and familiarity will become an important part of our relationship with God. We actually get to *know* this God whom we can trust with our life and our secret thoughts. Our trust is real, experiential and personal, not an intellectual idea about how to pray. Discernment then becomes more and more a natural outcome of our experience of God.

SUMMARY

As we look at the practice of discernment it becomes evident that it is partly *an acquired skill*, partly *dependence on God*, and partly *input from other members of the Body of Christ*. The truth is that we will always be limited in discerning what goes on in our own mind. Not only are we biased, but our vision is cloudy. So learning how to discern will therefore be an incremental process. We sense something, check with others about its validity, see the fruit, and become a bit more experienced in detecting the fingerprint of God. This in turn helps us make better sense of the next encounter, and so on.

With help and practice, we can learn to tell the difference between true discernment and telling ourselves what we think we want to hear. And as our discernment becomes sharper we will see more fruit in our life and more depth in our relationship with God.

Lord, I ask that You would attune our hearts to notice whatever things You want us to pay attention to, and that You would teach us to discern Your heart and Your voice. Keep us ever teachable and receptive, so that we can become more adept at following Your lead and trusting Your gifts to us. In Jesus' name ...

PERSONAL REFLECTION

What concerns do you still have regarding discernment? Do you know anyone who practices conversational prayer from whom you could ask for help in this area?

What are some examples of poor discernment you have seen in ministry?

DISCUSSION QUESTIONS

As you read through your journal entries, identify several places where you needed to discern the process and several where you had to discern the content. Share one of each type with your group.

What are some experiences you have had when God's word to you was particularly clear. How did you know it was him?

EXERCISE

One of the ways we can begin a conversation with God is to ask him a question about our own life. The particular question chosen for this exercise presents some interesting challenges in regard to discernment. For many people it will raise questions about what we want to hear and what we are afraid to hear, and ultimately about whether or not I am hearing from God. Try not to let these extra considerations generate any paralysis in your process, but instead trust that you can speak or write out what is in your heart at the moment and then later discern what part may be God's message to you.

Before proceeding, take a few moments to quiet and focus, and to let yourself rest in the presence of God.

Ask God the following question:

> *God, how do you see our relationship?*

If that question raises too much anxiety in you, or if your mind goes blank and you get nothing, then consider this question instead:

> *God, what do I need to know about your heart that would help me feel secure enough to ask you how you see our relationship?*

or possibly:

> *God, what can you tell me about the fear and defensiveness I feel when I think about asking you how you see our relationship?*

Feel free to express your own thoughts and feelings about your relationship with God, as well as any reactions you might have in regard to asking this kind of question.

Include whatever you sense God may be saying to you. Try not to guess what he would say, and try not to force it. Let it come to you. Write as you feel led, and when the stream slows down, ask God to help you see whatever may be genuinely his heart in the matter.

Chapter 8 – Responding

"Do not be like a man who looks at his face in a mirror and, after looking at himself, goes away and immediately forgets what he looks like" (Jas.1:23-24).

Responding actually refers to two different but related areas. First, we respond moment by moment as we continually discern what is happening in our time with God. Usually these responses are little more than making a change in direction or rephrasing a question. They are very much a part of how we participate actively and intentionally in our conversation.

But occasionally we will be led to respond in more significant ways, and especially as our conversation with God draws to a close. Whatever ways in which God has met us, blessed us, taught us, or healed us, we need to notice and embrace to the fullest extent possible. And that leads us to a very important question: *What can I take away with me from our time together, and how can I best hold onto it?*

If I have received some important insight, then I may want to find a way to internalize that new perspective more deeply. If my heart has been moved with gratitude, I may want to spend a few minutes allowing my appreciation toward God to flood my heart. Or if I have hit some dead ends in my reflection, I may need to spend a few more minutes outlining whatever still seems to be unresolved and in need of more discussion.

In any case, my response will probably fall into one of four major categories: Prayer, Quiet-Together, Action, or Sharing. We will take a closer look at each one of these areas.

Prayer

Perhaps the most common response to interacting with God is some form of prayer. Often our heart will gravitate very naturally toward prayer, as we reach out to hold onto what God has given us. We may feel led to give thanks, to intercede for a friend, or to ask for God's help in some part of our life.

If God has been talking to us about an area in which we need to make some changes, we may even be led to a prayer of repentance. Now in many Christian circles, repentance has become a term that is loaded with shame and condemnation. That is unfortunate, because repentance can be such a liberating experience when it is initiated by the Spirit of God.

We do not need to beat ourselves up in order to repent. Many of us already have enough trouble with shame due to a badly distorted self-image. All we really need is to see whatever God wants to show us and then run to him for help.

Keeping in mind that repentance is primarily a change of heart, we want to be careful not to fall back on our own resources for the solution. Many of us have been taught that repentance means, "I'm really sorry and I'll try harder, God, I promise!" But that is an approach to change that really does not work, because it depends on our own willpower.

Change comes from living in the presence of God and internalizing reality as God sees it, not from trying harder. Repentance is fundamentally an acknowledgment that *our way did not work*. So for us to attempt a course correction by our own resolve actually makes the same basic mistake all over again, because it is still trying to do things on our own. Only this time the error tries to hide under the disguise of attempting "righteous" behavior.

To put it another way, true repentance is a way of identifying a specific area in which we want God involved, and for which we desire *his* transforming hand. A better prayer of repentance might be something like this: "Lord I really do not want this part of me to have the kind of power that it has had in the past. I am powerless to change on my own, because I have tried and it has not worked. Let's talk about this so you can help me see what I have been missing, and then you can change my heart in regard to this thing." Such a prayer is an invitation for God to speak into my life and mentor me in his ways. The end result will be a change of mind that is far greater than anything I could have done by an act of the will alone.

We may also be led to a prayer of renunciation. Sometimes we come face to face with the realization that we have been actively participating in something that is harmful or evil. Turning away from that may require a deliberate pronouncement on our part that we will no longer accommodate that behavior or way of thinking in our soul.

This is not a magical formula for change, but a way of aligning with the right side of the battle in which we are engaged. Then we can receive more of what God wants to do in us to change our heart in ways that would not be possible if we remained ambivalent.

Suppose a father discovers that he has developed resentment toward his teenager because of the severity of the conflicts between them. Seeing that his anger is now part of the problem, he may need to renounce it out loud to God as a way of stating he will no longer be an active agent of destruction in his home. In doing so he aligns himself with the principles of life, and can then submit himself more fully to the rest of the work God wants to do in his mind and heart.

Spending a few minutes responding in prayer can make a big difference in how you internalize the things God has shown you in your time together.

Quiet-Together

When our conversation yields life-giving insights, or when we feel particularly close to God, it is good to let those thoughts and feelings "simmer" for a while, sinking deeper into our heart and mind. Spending time in quiet this way can feel a bit like "marinating" in the presence of God. Receive it as a gift and thank him for his care and love. This is very similar to David's process in Psalm 27 where he longed to spend time simply "beholding the beauty of the Lord."

Jesus promised us joy in his abiding presence, and we should receive it as a treasured gift to be savored and loved. That is why so much emphasis is seen in Paul's letters regarding the importance of *rejoicing and giving thanks*. Spending a few moments to allow the feelings of deep gratitude do their work is not a trivial exercise, but a vital part of our well-being.

Note that this is not about seeking an emotional experience for its own sake. This is simply an acknowledgment that the real presence of God often has an impact on our body and mind that we actually feel, and when it does, we want to receive it as a gift and rejoice in experiencing God's hand in our life.

Taking Concrete Actions to Internalize Truth

If during your reflections some word or thought has really captured your attention, you may want to write it down or find some way to hold on to it. I happen to have a ring that I wear on my right ring finger that says (in Hebrew), "I am my beloved's and my beloved is mine." One time after a particularly fruitful conversation with God over the phrase "You are not your own, you are bought with a price" (1Cor.6:19-20), I decided that when I put my ring on every morning I will say to myself, "You are not your own." That way, every day I have a moment where I stop and remember *whom I belong to*.

On another occasion, I was really taken by the phrase, "God is light, and in him is no darkness at all" (1Jn.1:5). What an incredible God to count on! So I searched my computer until I found a font in which the letters look a lot like little candles, and I printed out, "God is Light" in big letters and taped it on the wall where I was reminded for weeks about this beautiful part of God's nature. Capturing these phrases and doing what we can to help internalize them is an important part of responding.

Sometimes a passage has so much life in it that you may want to memorize a few verses so they stay with you better. One approach is to write them on a 3x5 card and carry it around with you. Pulling it out for review multiple times a day will help you remember the words as well as your conversation with God.

Finding concrete ways of responding can be a powerful way of internalizing truth and can go a long way toward helping us stay mindful of God's presence in our life. I would encourage you to be creative about finding such ways to respond. And if nothing comes to mind, ask God if he has any ideas about how you can hold on to his gifts to you.

Acts of Service to Others

Sometimes we need to connect our conversational prayer with the rest of our life. By actively investing in the lives of others, we become participants in the good that God is doing around us and learn more of what it means to be united with him in bringing life to our world. At the same time we place ourselves in positions where our weaknesses and unfinished areas will become exposed, giving us even more to talk to our Mentor about.

In most cases, these responses will come out of desire that God births in us to be with others and give them gifts that God has given us. This can be as simple as calling a friend, asking someone to coffee, taking a meal over to someone who is not feeling well, or writing a card to someone you care about. Or it may involve something more creative, such as working out a plan to give something to someone secretly, to bless them with God's love.

There are also times when God will lead us to extend ourselves beyond our comfort zone. For example, he may lay on your heart a desire to go down to the local rescue station and sign up for training in order to become an active volunteer. And when the weeks become long and volunteering gets hard, or when you find yourself disgusted with someone who comes for help, then you will have lots more that you can talk to your Father about so he can grow your heart to be more like his.

There are some places where Christians are goaded into service through shame, and even places where a spiritual hierarchy separates those who minster from those who are ministered to. I am not suggesting anything like that here. This is service from the heart, where God heals the minister as much as anyone else.

Sharing Our Journey with Others

Finally, we need to be deeply connected to other members of the Body, some of whom are upstream from us, some downstream, and some alongside us. By sharing part of what God reveals to us in our conversations, those upstream from us can rejoice with us, encourage us, and mentor us in our walk with God, while those alongside and downstream from us can be encouraged and be witnesses to the ways in which God works in those he loves.

In addition, sharing some of our reflections with others can help to anchor those experiences in our soul. By going over an encounter with God and expressing it in a way that is intelligible to another person, we internalize that experience and those insights even more.

SUMMARY

Learning how to respond to our time with God is an important part of engaging with him. Whether our response arises spontaneously or whether we have to quiet, listen, and discern in order to find a way to respond, we can internalize our time with God much more effectively when we take the time to act on the life we have received.

Lord, as I review my time with You, draw me to whatever would best serve to help me hold on to the gifts You have given me and absorb them deep into my heart. May they become a permanent part of what You are doing in my soul to mold me into the person You designed me to be. In Jesus' name...

Personal Reflection

If you look back over some of your earlier reflections, what are some additional ways that you could respond to those specific conversations?

Discussion Questions

What are some ways you have been led to respond?

How has this chapter changed your perceptions of what it might mean to actively participate in your own spiritual growth?

Exercise

Spend a few days working through Psalm 23. Even though this is a very familiar psalm, it has a lot of richness that can bring new life to even the most seasoned Christian.

Try finding a modern version that gives you a fresh perspective on the passage, and commit yourself to memorizing it.

Over a period of several days, take a different phrase from the psalm each day, and have a conversation with God about it, asking him to teach you more of what you need to see. Ask him to relate each phrase to some aspect of your life.

Recite the passage at night as you are falling asleep and try to recall some of the highlights of your conversations as you do.

Chapter 9 – When Hearing God is Difficult

"Now we see things imperfectly as in a cloudy mirror, but then we will see everything with perfect clarity. All that I know now is partial and incomplete" (1Cor.13:12 NLT).

While some people need little more than a nudge in the right direction in order to hear God speak to them, others seem to struggle a lot and can hardly sense God's voice at all. This can be quite disconcerting, and people may wonder if they are doing something wrong or if God is holding out on them for some reason. So with that in mind we turn to the issue of providing additional help to those who would like to hear from God but seem to be unable to connect very well.

It might be reassuring to know that even those who find conversations with God to be fairly natural can experience difficulty hearing from time to time. No one has a consistently clear connection. Problems can vary from being uncertain about what we are receiving, to feeling lost, to sensing absolutely nothing at all. But none of these issues represent a moral failure on our part or any reluctance on God's part to engage with us. With a little help, most of us can reconnect with God and begin hearing from him again.

We will begin with some of the more common barriers and proceed to some of the more difficult problems we can face (though the order is not precise). If you are having trouble sensing God's promptings, please consider the following areas to see if they can point you in the right direction. Above all, be persistent. Your life is worth the effort.

Being Too Passive

One of the most common problems is that of being too passive in the process of listening. To empty our mind and wait quietly for God to capture our attention and say something may seem like the right way to proceed. But the problem is that this approach leaves us far too disengaged. Conversational prayer is a two-way process in which we generally do better if we can learn how to listen as we talk with God.

Many Christians have in their mind a picture of hearing God that is something along the lines of how God spoke to Samuel when he was a little boy. God called him in such a distinct and clear manner that Samuel mistook God's voice for the old priest Eli. God interrupted Samuel's sleep and got his attention without any effort on Samuel's part to seek him out. We see similar patterns in several other Bible stories in which God sends an archangel or interjects himself in some other way that cannot be missed by those to whom he is speaking. So it might be easy to think that this is the way God usually speaks to us and we should just be still and wait for his voice to interrupt our silence.

However, this is *not* the pattern that we generally see portrayed in the Psalms, or even in the life of Jesus (who listened to his Father all the time). Nor is it how most saints through the ages have described their experience of God. While he is certainly capable of speaking audibly or through some special spiritual gifting, this is not the way in which he usually mentors his people. As discussed earlier, we most often experience God's communication in the form of impressions and spontaneous thoughts. And the most effective way to perceive these impressions is to be engaged in the conversation as active participants and not just passive recipients.

For most people then, *spending time in focused reflection* is a very effective bridge to hearing God. Reflecting deeply on a verse or a life issue that is meaningful to us engages our mind and heart, and enables us to become more receptive to God. But just to be clear, when we use the term *spiritual reflection* we are not talking about a purely cognitive exercise of our rational capacities. Our body, soul, heart, and mind all need to be involved in the process as we look for God's participation with us.

For example, suppose we decide to reflect on the gifts in our life for which we can be grateful. One approach would be to start a list on a piece of paper and try to see how many things we can think of, as though it were some kind of test. But at that point we are still barely engaging our mind and heart. What we need to do is take each item that comes to mind and let it become real to us, remembering how it felt to receive it, and savoring its value to us as we picture it in our mind. Allowing our heart to rejoice over each gift touches our deepest appreciation for God, stirs our longings for more of him in our life, and brings us closer to a spirit of receptivity, an openness to receive whatever he might have for us.

Thus, as we learn how to ruminate on the things of God with our whole heart, we see things in a way we have not seen before, discover places inside where we need more healing, and we begin to notice that not all of our thoughts have the same weight or impact on our soul. As we become familiar with the way God breathes life into our very being, we come to expect God's active presence within us. Our relationship grows with our conversations into a way of life that we come to enjoy more and more.

All of this is quite deliberate on our part, to seek after the things which God has put in our heart to desire, and to actively reflect on them for all they are worth, turning them over and over in our mind until they yield up the gems which they hold for us. In this way we prepare our heart to receive, and we will begin to notice more and more the impressions we are receiving from God.

Not Recognizing God's Spirit

A friend of mine was sharing an entry from his journal with me which included a significant breakthrough for him regarding an issue with which he was wrestling. Then he added, "But I did not have any real sense that God was speaking to me."

I asked him what else he could tell me about his experience right at the moment in which he grasped the new insight. He said it felt as if he had taken a breath of fresh air. I told him, "That, my friend, is your soul responding to the life that was in those words, and that is one of the ways you can know that it is God who is speaking to you."

Sometimes the problem is not that a person is having trouble hearing from God, but rather that they do not recognize God's voice for what it is. If we are expecting something overly dramatic like an audible voice or fully formed sentences ringing in our mind, then we may miss the more subtle ways in which he normally speaks.

When God communicates with us Spirit-to-spirit, we often experience that message as an intuitive leap, a highly relevant memory, a heart-felt song, a spontaneous thought, or a meaningful new insight into what we are discussing with him. It may or may not strike us as a fully formed thought. We may only have a partially formed idea that we need to pursue a few moments more before we find the words for our impression. But we usually feel as if our soul is taking in a drink of cool, clear water. God himself talks about his word to us as a feast for the soul (Isa.55).

The more life-giving the thought and the more fruitful it is in our mind and heart, the more we can be certain that it is a thought given to us by God. These elements can vary greatly, from a minor glimmer of hope, to a grateful heart, to bursting with joy. But the very nature of the things God reveals to us means that they will usually be accompanied by some fruit of the Spirit, such as love, joy, peace, or experiential truth. This is not a "prophetic utterance" or other kind of event where we would expect a sign or audible voice, but the quiet teaching of a very wise Rabbi *with* whom we desire to be, and *from* whom we have an interest in grasping a better view of the unseen world.

Recognizing God's revelations can take time. So be patient with yourself as you learn what is from him. Find another person who is familiar with hearing God and talk to them about what you are experiencing. They may be able to help you with your discernment in these matters.

Personal Disbelief

One of the more subtle issues that can hinder us from participating with God's work in us is a kind of personal disbelief that many struggle with. This is not the same thing as an intellectual form of disbelief that we hear from those whose theology will not allow them to believe God talks to people today. What I mean by *personal* disbelief is that voice inside that says, "God never talks to *me*. He may talk to you, he may talk to Christians generally. But I don't think he will ever talk to *me*. Or if he does, I will probably never hear him."

The doubter may not even think of this as disbelief. It just feels true. For whatever reason, they have dismissed the possibility of anything that personal happening between them and God, at least for the time being. Either God does not really care to talk to them, or there is something in them that is so spiritually bereft that they will not be able to hear what God says to them. They may even be afraid to try listening for God, because the disappointment of not hearing is too painful to bear over and over.

This can be a tremendous barrier, because hope feels like such a dangerous thing. If I try to hear from God but hear nothing, my heart will be crushed. It feels like rejection. If I have to endure the lack of connection, I would rather do it without the added pain of rejection by God or repeated failure on my part.

What we need to understand is that we are not alone in this. However we arrived at this disbelief regarding God's voice, we are in good company. Some get to this place because of self-hate or self-rejection. "If you knew me better you would not like me or want to be near me, so why would God give me the time of day when he knows me better than anyone else? If I'm disappointed in me, certainly God must be disappointed. That would only make sense. And since I will not be able change who I am any time soon, I really don't expect him to talk to me."

Others reach this place of disbelief simply because they have always felt distant from God. They may have wanted a closer connection with God at one time, but they never got any sense that he was anywhere nearby. With no one to help them build an experiential relationship, they eventually settled for the hope that things will be better when they die and see him face to face. For now, about all they can expect is an occasional warm fuzzy feeling on Sunday morning. Talk about hearing God sounds nice, but it also sounds too remote to ever be a part of their life.

What all of these experiences have in common is a subtle form of disbelief that is, more than anything else, a problem with trust. Dallas Willard calls this our "broken truster". We have reached the point where we can no longer believe enough to get past our fear. A broken truster is not something we can fix through our own effort or by an act of our will. Instead, we need to build a relationship with someone who is good enough to trust, so we can let down our guard and receive without fear whatever goodness may come from them. With that kind of experience, our truster can be healed.

But that sounds a lot like a catch-22. I need to connect with God in order to heal my truster. But I cannot connect with him very well because my truster is broken. So no matter what our theology tells us, what *feels true* is that it is God himself who is not trustworthy.

The first step to resolving this dilemma is to understand that there is no shame in having a broken truster. One of the reasons God came to restore us to wholeness was because we have all been wounded by life in a broken world and are in need of God's healing hand. By coming to terms with our brokenness, we can begin to accept the truth that God is indeed trustworthy, even if it does not feel like it at the moment. *That in and of itself then becomes an act of trust in God's goodness.*

That small bit of trust can then lead us to some of the healing we need, which in turn will lead to more trust, more healing, and so on. This may not happen overnight, but it does happen, because God can do great things with what little trust we are capable of.

We can also foster this healing by taking steps to deepen our expectation of God's goodness in our life. One such practice is to turn our thoughts to the goodness of God for five or ten minutes each morning as we are waking up and each night as we are going to sleep.

This practice is not at all as trivial as it might sound. If we allow our heart to appreciate the goodness of God for even a few minutes a day, it will begin seeping into the depths of our being, giving us hope that God will speak into our life. Because once we are convinced in our soul that God is good enough to trust, we can begin to open up to him in ways that would not be possible from a place of fear.

Finally, we must never condemn ourselves for having doubts about hearing from God. Such disbelief does not arise in a vacuum, but has ample reason for forming in our heart. We must simply take it back to God, lift it up in faith to him and say,

"Look, Daddy! See what else I found broken? Can we fix it? Can we begin now? I really want this fixed so we can be closer. Please show me what I need to know so we can work on this together."

As one New Testament writer put it, "Those who come to God must believe that he is with them and that he responds to those who actively seek him" (Heb.11:6, paraphrased). No matter what our prior experience has been or how much we doubt today that God will talk to us, we need to commit whatever we can to God and ask him to heal us and help us through the rest. If we will believe in faith that God wants this relationship even more than we do, and that a way actually exists for this to become a reality in our life, then we can commit to learning how to engage with him and allow him to restore our trust, piece by piece.

Anger at God

Without meaning to, many people are actually opposed to receiving from God on an emotional level, despite their genuine desire to hear from him. Emotional resistance to God is not something we ordinarily choose to harbor, but rather it comes out of various life experiences in which we internalized some distorted perceptions of God. We will look here at three of the most common forms of emotional resistance – anger, shame, and fear.

Being *angry at God* is surprisingly common. Predominately, people are angry with him because of something that happened to them that he did not prevent. They may have been raised by terribly deficient (or downright evil) parents; they may have been involved in an accident; or perhaps they got cancer or some other life-threatening disease. Whatever the reason, they look around and see others who have not had to go through the things they have endured and feel as if God has been particularly hard on them, if not mean or even punitive. If God would let them go through such terrible things, they do not feel as if they can trust him with their life or build any sort of meaningful relationship with him.

A related source of anger arises from having prayers that seem to go unanswered and from not receiving the good things that people believe God should have given them. Among the more difficult issues are those having to do with asking God year after year for deliverance from some problem without seeing anything change. Even though there may be every reason to believe God would be in favor of such a deliverance based on the good news we see in Scripture, people find themselves trapped in addictions, bad marriages, and all sorts of problems that do not seem to change through prayer. It is not too hard to see how someone could arrive at the conclusion that God does not care much for them.

Of course it will be impossible here to resolve either the problem of evil in the world or the matter of unanswered petitions to God. But let me offer two thoughts on this. First, regarding the physical world in which we live and the great many things that go wrong in our lives, the Bible is quite open about the fact that believers will experience hardship and even death. One only needs to read Hebrews 11 to get a glimpse of the things saints have endured over the centuries. So whatever world view we try to put together in order to make sense of the pain we experience, we need to be realistic about what it means to live in a broken world. As Christians we are not immune to its effects.

If we try to develop a theology in which we are protected from harm because we believe in God, we put our faith in a false hope that will only lead to an eventual collapse of our faith. We cannot with any integrity blame God for not living up to our wishful thinking.

Second, in regard to spiritual issues that we pray about without seeing any results, we must come to see that the problem is not a matter of God's lack of response, but of the lack of understanding that characterizes much of the Christian world in regard to how spiritual restoration actually takes place. The sad truth is that relatively few Christians really know how to help people grow up spiritually or how to help them recover from life's problems when willpower alone is not enough to bring about change. So the average Christian can easily exhaust all of the known resources and be left with the impression that the only missing element is God's response. But the truth is that we have not been taught how to engage with God in ways that can reach the deep inner needs of our heart. That is why we need a book like this present one to help us connect with God in a tangible way.

What *can* we say about being angry at God over how our life is turning out? While it may *feel true* that the problem lies with God, that he is too distant or holding out on us, the truth is that we simply are not in possession of all that we need to know in order to move forward. If we could see what he sees, we would be able to find the resolution we need and we would no longer have reason to be angry at him. Ironic as it may be, the only way to find out what he knows and what we do not, is to learn how to engage with him and hear his voice so he can teach us about our own life. We may simply have to give God the benefit of the doubt and move ahead in faith, believing that he can eventually show us what is missing from our view of things.

Fear of God

Another form of emotional resistance that many Christians face (strange as it may be for a faith that is based on God's love) is a significant *fear of God* which they harbor in their heart. We are not talking about the kind of fear that is a form of awe or reverence, but an unholy fear that makes us want to keep our distance from God and hold him at arm's length.

Fear of God presents itself in a lot of ways:

- Afraid of getting too close (I might get overwhelmed)
- Afraid of getting too far away (he might leave me)
- Afraid of what he thinks of me (he knows way too much)
- Afraid of what he might do to me (he might test me)
- Afraid of not knowing what his will is (I might miss it and be judged for that)
- Afraid of finding out what his will is (he might want too much from me)

What all of these fears have in common is a distrust of God because of what we believe about his character and about his ways of interacting with people. Again, it usually *feels true* that God is scary and cannot be relied upon to have the same ideas we have about what makes life good.

Quite often these fears can be traced to the influence of untrustworthy caregivers in a person's early years who could never be counted on for goodness. When reinforced by bad theology that makes God out to be a highly judgmental being who does not like them very much, it is not too hard to see why such a person might be afraid of him.

I do not mean to be repetitious, but once again the real problem is not that God is actually untrustworthy but rather that our perceptions and beliefs about him are terribly distorted due to our faulty interpretations of life experience in a fallen world. The truth is that the problem lies with our broken "truster" and not the object of our trust. If we would experience God as he truly is our fears would become a vapor and melt away.[11]

That is not to say this is an easy issue to deal with, just that in order to overcome our fear of God we need to believe that the

---

[11] Paul's prayer in Ephesians 3 essentially says, "If you could just get how much God really loves you, it would completely change your life."

problem is actually inside us. We need to approach God in spite of our fear, with the understanding that once we get to know him well enough we will no longer be afraid of how he will treat us. In fact, acting on the belief that the better we know him the more we will love him and not fear him, is itself an act of trust that he is in truth, a trustworthy God.

Shame and Self-Rejection

The third emotional barrier to engaging with God is *shame*. Some of us feel so much shame that it feels impossible to get close to God. I know all the secret things about myself that I hate, so God must know them, too, and feel the same way about them that I do. If I am disappointed in myself, certainly God is disappointed. Getting close to God just shines the light on how bad I am, and it feels so ugly I want to hide from him.

When these feelings come from a place of deep self-rejection or self-hate, it can feel intensely true that God must be disgusted with me, that he would not want to be with me, and that he certainly would not want to talk to me about anything other than how I need to get myself cleaned up. Unfortunately, I am such a mess I *cannot* get cleaned up, so I have no hope of ever getting God to like me well enough to have a decent relationship. Whenever I try to have a conversation with God, all I hear are the old tapes running through my head telling me all the things that are wrong with me.

While all of this may feel very true, the reality is far different. God is not a judgmental God who gives pass-fail tests, nor a God of condemnation who keeps track of all your failings, nor a God who hates you when you come in with anything less than perfect performance.

Rather, he is a Father who delights in rescuing and restoring his children. "Blessed are the spiritually impoverished, because they get to be in the Kingdom, too!" (Mt.5:3 paraphrased). We do not have to earn the right to be in relationship with him. Instead he comes to live in us and offer us a relationship that has enough substance to change us so that we can become the kind of people he created us to be. Grace means we get the relationship first, and then we can work on the stuff in the context of that relationship!

He knows we are made of dust, that we are jars of clay. That is no surprise to him. He does not sit there and shake his head when we make mistakes. Rather, he gives us his Spirit to guide and mentor us in life so that we can become more and more Christ-like.

Which is to say that all of our self-hate is entirely founded on a pile of lies about who we are, who God is, and how this whole relationship thing works. Yes, there are a lot of preachers out there who would like to make you feel like a miserable sinner and tell you that shame keeps you humble. But that is a very poor caricature of the good news. And self-castigation is really not a Christian virtue or a fruit of the Spirit.

If we will in faith approach God in spite of our shame and seek to get to know him through conversational prayer, we will discover a God who loves us far more than we could ever imagine, with a love that is big enough to break through all of our self-hate and shame, bringing us healing and relief.

What all these forms of emotional resistance have in common is a distrust of God's goodness, which invariably is rooted in a distorted sense of who God is and how he might interact with us. With each of these barriers, I have suggested that our best hope for resolving these issues is to move closer to God instead of trying to protect ourselves from him. But I do not mean to trivialize the power these emotional issues may have in us. In many cases we may need to seek out others who have a conversational relationship with God and ask for their help.

Relational Blocks and Other Problems Related to
the Right-Hemisphere of the Brain

One final area needs to be mentioned with regard to the kinds of things that can get in the way of having fruitful conversations with God, and that is how our physical brain and our neurological processes are related to sensing and hearing God. Addressing this area is important, because it highlights a problem that has not received a lot of attention. However, if you identify heavily with this issue you will need to find outside resources for resolution, because adequate coverage would lie beyond the scope of a book such as this. I will limit my treatment here to a brief description of the problem and a few comments regarding the direction for help.

Given that we are embodied spiritual beings, we need to acknowledge that our spiritual life is deeply intertwined with our physical and mental health. Each affects the other. Just as genuine joy can improve our immune system and spiritual renewal can improve how our mind works, so also taking certain types of drugs or incurring certain injuries to the brain can significantly impact our spiritual well-being. But the connections go much farther.

In particular, our brain contains a number of circuits that govern our perceptions and regulate our involvement whenever we have a conversation with another person. Some of these circuits monitor the subtle non-verbal cues that accompany our interaction, some attempt to see the conversation from the other person's point of view, some keep track of how we ourselves are impacting the relational dynamics between us, and still others allow us to feel connected, to value the other person and to feel valued. These brain circuits all work together to provide us with the ability to participate well in a conversation, to listen attentively and accurately, to relate to the other person in life-giving ways, and to create a rich experience for both of us (Wilder and Khouri).

Unfortunately, these relational circuits do not always function as well as God designed them to. We have all seen someone who has become so overwhelmed by their situation that they begin to treat people around them like problems to be fixed or removed. The classic case is that of a drowning person who tries to use their rescuer as a floatation device. But we have all done that to a lesser degree in times when we have been overrun by emotion.

One of the things that is happening during such an event is that the person's relational circuits are shutting down. They may stop seeing other people as valuable, or even as human beings. Most likely they will stop noticing how they themselves are involved in the deterioration of the relationship, but instead blame all of the problems on someone or something else. After they calm down and their relational circuits begin working again, they may feel a great deal of remorse and wonder how they could have behaved in such a manner.

Many of us could also name a person we know who seems to be impaired in this way most of the time. We might even say that "they do not have a relational bone in their body." They rarely notice how they are impacting other people, and for the most part what impact they do have is rough and disconcerting. Our tendency is to keep our distance and find reasons to not be around them for very long.

What is going on there? For whatever reason, their relational circuits are not functioning well. Causes can range anywhere from ingesting too many harmful drugs, to physical brain injuries, to various forms of emotional abuse and/or neglect in childhood. Actually a wide variety of possibilities exist for this condition. And what's more, this kind of impairment can go from barely perceptible to severely disturbing and everything in between. In fact, no one has all of their relational circuits working perfectly all the time.

The point is that we use most of these same relational circuits when we try to sense the presence of God and have conversations with him. The more our relational circuits have been damaged, the more difficulty we will have paying attention to God's Spirit and hearing what he has to say to us.

Now this might not sound very "spiritual" and one might wonder why we need these particular brain circuits working in order to engage in conversational prayer. But we cannot separate our mindful processes from the gray matter that we use for perceiving and thinking and feeling. If our relational circuits are working poorly in regard to other people, we will most likely have trouble hearing clearly from the Spirit as well.

So what can be done for those who are suffering from a mind that is malfunctioning? In broad terms, they are in need of some corrective experiences that can help to wake up those circuits. For many people, a few minutes of quiet with some attention given to genuinely appreciating the gifts and goodness of God can dramatically increase their relational capacities. For others who have experienced more significant damage to their relational circuits, they may need to seek out the help of a trained counselor or mentor to work on these issues.

Summary

Wherever you are having difficulty hearing from God, be sure to spend some time reflecting on the nature of the barrier you are experiencing and invite God to join you in your pondering. See if any of the areas in this chapter describe what you are dealing with, and talk to God about what you need from him in order to move forward. If necessary, find someone else who can help you.

Restoring our connection to God is vital to our spiritual life. Whatever is in the way, you can be sure it is worth the risk and the effort to reengage with him.

For Those Who Are Discouraged

For whatever reason, there are some people who seem to have great difficulty sensing anything from God, no matter how much they try to hear from him.

Usually accompanied by no small discouragement, this problem may be taken quite personally in one of two ways. From their perspective, either God *is* talking to them and they cannot hear him because of some defect in their listening, or God is *not* talking to them because they are doing something wrong. Either way they feel rejected and cannot understand why God does not break through the barriers and speak more clearly. These feelings may become painful enough to cause some people to stop trying altogether.

Without trying to minimize how discouraging this might be, my hope is that if you are having trouble hearing God you will not despair or give up. Of all the things you have ever tried to do that were hard for you, this one is most worth your efforts and holds the most promise for goodness in your life. I cannot tell you how much this has changed my life or how much poorer I would be if I had not persisted in learning how to have conversations with God.

For those who struggle, there is always the question of why this is so hard when it is supposed to be the birthright of every child of God, and why it is so easy for others who seem to hear so clearly. While I will try to offer some thoughts in regard to why you should continue to pursue this, I cannot say I know for certain why some people have so much trouble. I only know that the more you persist, the more likely you will experience the breakthrough you so desire.

Perhaps the single most valuable thing a person can do in this situation is to seek out a mature Christian who is able to hear

God, a person who is grace-filled, patient, and themselves teachable and growing in spiritual things. If no one comes to mind, ask a few trusted friends to read this book and work through it together with them. When some of the members of your group begin to hear God in ways that are genuinely fruitful, see what they can do to encourage and mentor the rest of you. God gave us the body of believers for just such a reason as this. Ask him to help you find the people that can help you learn.

Remember, too, that conversational prayer is very much a learned process. Earlier we referred to the analogy of learning to play the violin. At first, the noise that comes out of that instrument barely resembles music at all. But with time and patience, a student can learn to hold the bow just so and apply the right pressure and press the strings in the right place, and music will begin to flow.

Another analogy might be seen in how young children acquire language. Initially, infants do not even know that the sounds made by mom and dad have any distinct meaning at all. As they continue to pay attention, certain words begin to connect with their world and they can even pick a few of them out of a string of other words they do not know yet. Gradually their vocabulary grows, along with complex syntax and various word endings that can alter the meanings of words.

Similarly, learning to pay attention to the movements of the Spirit in our heart takes some time and persistence. At first we may only realize after the fact that God was somehow involved in our reflection, because we feel as if our soul has been fed. Our early attempts to discern where to go and how to proceed may often take us to unproductive places. Only with repeated attempts will we learn how to tell a prompting of the Spirit from an internal distraction. But gradually we will learn how to focus our attention, how to ruminate about a thought and watch for any leading at the same time, how to seek depth instead of breadth, and to deal with many other matters as well.

All of this leads us back to the value of practicing spiritual reflection on a regular basis. I would encourage those who are not discerning much from God to continue writing out their thoughts and feelings as they ponder passages of Scripture or wrestle with life issues. Not only is this a valuable practice on its own due to its inherent focus, but spiritual reflection is one of the best ways to build a bridge to hearing directly from God.

The point is that we need to seek God with our whole heart and soul, and we need to persist in that seeking until the treasure is realized. Know that God is seeking you, too, and that he intends for your good and for your heart to know him more. May God bless your persistence and desire to connect with him in this way.

Lord, only You know why we fail to hear Your voice and what we need in order to recover the relationship that You intend for us to have. Help us. Encourage us. Give us the hope we need to pursue You. And reveal to us in Your love what we need to see in order to move closer to You in this process. Thank You for Your patience and persistence. In Jesus' name ...

Personal Reflection

What things do you identify with in this chapter?

What do you want to try in relation to dealing with these areas?

Discussion Questions

When have you been angry with God? Afraid of him?
Too ashamed to be near him?
How have you dealt with these feelings in the past?

What are some concrete examples of being non-relational in our interactions with others? In our interactions with God?

If you find it hard to believe that God will speak to you, what are your reasons for believing this?

Exercise

If you identify with any of the problems outlined in this chapter, please try the following.

1. Spend a few minutes quieting and focusing.
2. Use your appreciation list (see exercise in ch.5) to stir up your awareness of God's goodness.
3. Ask God to help you understand your area of difficulty, and begin writing to him what you see.
4. Continue writing as you feel led, and see if God can shed some light on what you are wrestling with.
5. Share your experience with another person.

Chapter 10 – Reaping the Rewards

"I pray that the God of our Lord Jesus Christ ... may give you a spirit of wisdom and revelation as you come to know him" (Eph.1:17).

How Much Time?

"How much time does it take to have a fruitful conversation with God?"

When people begin to learn about conversational prayer, this is one of the most common questions they have. It is a reasonable question, but one that does not necessarily have a simple answer.

If I suggest spending an hour a day, many people will say that is impossible and give up before they ever find out how wonderful this way of prayer can be. If I say you only need ten minutes, most people will find that nothing much happens in ten minutes and give up for lack of fruit. So let me say it this way. My hope is that you will not only try this approach to engaging with God, but that you will do whatever it takes until your conversational relationship with God has become fruitful and satisfying.

At the same time, I understand that a few guidelines might be helpful. Please be aware that I am about to make some sweeping generalizations based on my own experience and that of a few others over the last few years.

Generally speaking, people spend the first ten minutes or so getting focused and personally invested in their conversation, regardless of whether it is about a passage of Scripture or a life issue. During the next ten to twenty minutes, much of the fruit begins to show up. God may breathe life into a particular phrase, he may give them a new insight that brings a sense of peace, or he may simply encourage them or lead them to bask in the beauty of his presence for a while. And for most people most of the time, that is sufficient. That means somewhere between twenty and thirty minutes might be a relatively good target for those who are learning to have conversations with God.

Of course, obstacles or other special circumstances could affect the quality of our prayer time. For example, if I am asking God to renew my mind in regard to an old self-defeating life pattern or emotional scar, I might need to dig around for thirty or forty minutes just to discover the true source of my pain, and then work with God for a while longer before I am able to receive from him what I need for healing. Or if I am having a terribly bad day and I need to connect with him for the sake of keeping my sanity, I may very well spend most of my time just trying to quiet down enough to have any sense of his presence with me.

On the other hand, if I am in a really good place I might need no more than a single glance at my last journal entry to bring me back to where we left off. Within seconds I may find myself surrounded by God, receiving new gifts from him. So the time we need in order to have a fruitful conversation can vary quite a bit.

Then, too, just as it is good to get away once in a while with your spouse or a friend, from time to time we also need to make space for a personal retreat with God. It could be for an afternoon or for an entire weekend. These extended times with him allow us to go much deeper, and for God to impact our heart and mind much more profoundly. That does not mean we will spend an entire retreat in complete rapture. Usually there is an ebb and flow to our time together, and a kind of rhythm between alternating periods of intensity and rest. We may go from deeply moving experiences of God to quiet walks through nature or taking a nap.

I am sure that for many people, even carving out twenty or thirty minutes a day sounds like too much time. But let me suggest something. Rather than cutting your conversations down to ten minutes in an attempt to do it every day, try setting aside thirty minutes three times a week so that you can get the depth you need. Or spend even more time on your day off, if possible. That way you are giving this approach to engaging with God a real chance of feeding your soul sufficiently to experience its true value.

Once you get a taste of what it is like to be with God, you will not want to go without.

What Can We Expect to Receive From God?

Throughout this book I have given many real life examples of what God may do in our conversations with him that will bring life to our spirit and substance to our soul. But before we end, I would like to make a point of the kinds of things we can expect to receive from him.

Expect Clarification and Insight

Having someone as great as the Creator of Life for a Mentor means that he can show us things we have never seen before, as well as show us greater significance in many things we are already familiar with.

Reading through the book of Matthew, I was captivated by the first Beatitude where Jesus said, "Blessed are the poor in spirit, for theirs is the Kingdom of heaven" (Mt.5:3). Now, I have never cared much for the common interpretation which reads the passage as "Once you know you are poor, you can then enter the Kingdom." I think that completely misses Jesus' intention.

So my first step was to ask God to help me paraphrase the verse into something that would make better sense to me. What came to mind was, *"Blessed are the spiritually impoverished, because they get to be in the Kingdom, too!"* I liked that, because it better captures the spirit of the good news Jesus was announcing. He was offering the Kingdom to broken people. "How blessed are you who are so far down the wrong path you would never be able to enter on the basis of your own merit. The availability of the Kingdom does not depend on your performance, but on My grace and my desire to be with you!"

But then I asked what seemed like an obvious question. "Lord, if your Kingdom is the place where your will is done, then how can spiritually impoverished people be in your Kingdom? How can they be *in your will?"*

After a few moments of wondering how God might view spiritually poor people, I realized that if they were in the Kingdom very long, they would grow and heal. So I began to envision what it might be like for them to be changed by their new life. At that point I was hit by a sudden insight. "My Kingdom is not about perfection, it is about *restoration!* My will is to restore people to wholeness. So all those who are in need of restoration qualify."

That beautifully clarified some very important matters for me. God's Kingdom *is* wherever his will is being carried out. Amazingly, we can be truly impoverished and in God's will at the same time, because our restoration is precisely what his will is about! That insight drew me closer to God and made me even more grateful and hopeful about his involvement in my life.

Clarifications and insights like this are common in our conversations with God. He wants us to know how life works in the Kingdom, how much he cares for us, who we are in his eyes, where we need to go next, and so on. All of these things become more clear as we engage with him for his light of truth.

Expect Reinterpretations of Our Own Life Experience

Having a Mentor who can help us see life as God sees it makes all the difference in the world. Given that his ways are higher than our ways we can assume that no matter what we are considering, we have to be missing something! That is why one of the best questions we can ask God is, "What am I missing here?" A very real example of this can be seen in the life of someone I know whom we will refer to as Daniel.

For nearly fifty years, Daniel had held deep resentments toward his parents and several of his siblings because of his early family life. This issue had come to the surface on many occasions and Daniel had prayed, cried, repented, and done everything he could think of to let go of his anger and hate. But every time he was in the same room with some of those family members, all the feelings of resentment would come flooding back and it was all he could do just to clench his jaw shut and remain civil.

One day God gave Daniel a picture of his family out in about twelve feet of water with everyone thrashing around trying to get some air. In order to breathe, each person would grab the one next to them and push them under, and they in turn would get pushed down by someone else. As Daniel contemplated the image, it suddenly dawned on him, "They're not being mean… they're desperate!" The revelation broke his heart, and he never again felt his previous level of bitterness and hate. Instead, he felt compassion for them and longed for their healing. Once God reframed his understanding of his family, Daniel's heart changed and his resentments died.

This way of healing our wounds is an important part of why we need to connect with God and receive his truth deep into our soul. As we learn how to bring our brokenness to God and hear his penetrating truth, we can be set free of many of the things that keep us in bondage and can then live more the way God intended.

Not all of our reinterpretations need to be this dramatic. God can take even simple misunderstandings or hurt feelings and give us a bigger picture that helps to make sense of things.

One day I got rather irritated with my wife because it seemed like she was leaving an unpleasant task to me that we had agreed to do together. I no sooner began to talk to God about my anger than he virtually interrupted me with, "She is really overbooked right now and needs your help." The situation was completely obvious once I saw it, but I had been quite blind to that perspective before.

Since I know what it is like to be overbooked – I've been there myself – my resentment dissipated very quickly, and I began to seek out ways to help her lighten the weight of her schedule. As a result of our discussions she eventually extracted herself from a part-time job that had been very draining and taking her away from her growing ministry focus. Once I saw what I had not seen before, new avenues of resolution opened up that bore fruit in both our lives.

We need to learn how to see life through the eyes of heaven. Spending time with God and asking him to reveal what we do not see, is an important part of being an apprentice of the Kingdom.

Expect to See More of His Heart and Character

Sometimes directly, sometimes indirectly, God will reveal himself to us in many ways.[12] Over time, we get to know more of who he is through our experience of him. We discover how much he wants our restoration and how much he enjoys being with us. By the gentle ways he confronts us, we learn that he is not disgusted by who we are, but rather that he is incredibly understanding and patient with us as we relearn how to live. This

---

[12] "I will love them and reveal myself to them." (Jn.14:21).

in turn means that it is completely safe to go to him with all of our failures and brokenness and ask for his help.

I am reminded again of the time I asked God about the phrase, "to whom much is given, much is required." As I approached him I was feeling a lot of shame about how poorly I had dealt with what I have been given. Gently, God told me to stop beating myself up about that because there was no way I would ever keep up with his ability to give good gifts. His desire was to give me more than I can receive, let alone fully use. So while there were still things for us to talk about in regard to my use of his gifts, I did not have to be burdened by his generosity.

Experiences like that have helped me to see more of God's character, which in turn has allowed me to trust him more with my deepest shame and failures. I know he will help me and not condemn me. He really does have my best interest at heart. And while I always "believed" that theologically, I now know it first-hand, in a way that is deeply, emotionally reassuring.

Expect to See More of the Secrets of Our Own Heart

Of course, the closer we get to the Light, the more our flaws will show up. Fortunately for us, the closer we are to God the less we will be *condemned* by those flaws. As our relationship with God continues to grow and we learn how to bring our messiness to him, we discover how to let down our defenses in his presence. Things then often come to the surface that we may have had little if any awareness of before.

For example, any lack of trust in God's provision for us or any belief in the scarcity of good things will become evident in the light of his goodness, and problems we thought we had solved will resurface in new and unexpected ways. But through it all, God holds us in his heart and takes care with each new revelation to heal and mentor us through our restoration.

Much like a master painter might gently correct a novice's use of color, texture, and light, the Holy Spirit shows us what we need to know about our own character, and then does the work of repair, because we cannot do that on our own. We can actually become quite accustomed to God's confrontations. Even when he is quite bold about it, he confronts us with such grace that it is never harmful. I may not like what I see in myself, but I have complete confidence that God knows what to do about it and that I will not always be the way I am right now. With all of that as a foundation, I am completely safe as he opens my heart for healing.

Since God is committed to our restoration, it is necessary from time to time for him to expose our brokenness so that we can cooperate in the process. Although the healing is his work and not ours, he requires our conscious participation, often in the form of extended conversations with him. Allowing him to bring those issues to the surface is part of how we submit to his work within us. We can be sure that he will do his part in both revealing and healing our life issues.

The Long Term Impact of Conversational Prayer

Conversational prayer has done more to change my life in the last ten years than all the other things I tried to do in the first forty years of my Christian life. Spending time with God, listening to his heart, and learning to hear his wisdom and to be cared for by his words to me has profoundly changed my life.

Nothing I have ever done for ministry, nothing I have ever heard or experienced in Christian conferences, nothing I learned in my theological studies – *nothing* compares to what God has done in my heart and mind in those quiet moments when we talk heart to heart.

If it were only insight that we received from conversational prayer day after day, that would be reason enough to practice this way of connecting with our heavenly Mentor. But that is only the beginning of the rewards that come from engaging with God.

First, we get to *know* God personally in a way that is vastly different from knowing *about* God. To be known and loved by God is how we were designed to live, and the only thing that will fill those holes in our heart where we need to be loved enough to make a difference.

As important as good theology is, having real conversations with God is the kind of direct contact that gives us food for our soul and life for our body. Learning experientially how he cares for me, how he speaks to me, what he wants for me, are all part of getting to know who this amazing God really is. Our relationship becomes a reality with substance, far beyond our theology and the ideas we have about him. He is good beyond our best hopes. And nothing is better than knowing him first hand.

Second, engaging with the Author of Life brings about healing and transformation like nothing else. The wounds we carry around and the sins that plague our life begin to lose their power, one after another, as we learn how to present these things to God for the truth and light that only he can provide. God's voice carries with it the power of Life. And receiving his Light and Life into our heart is the most freeing experience in the world.

The single most important thing about the Christian life is the quality of our relationship with God. And one of the strongest indicators of our relationship with God is the quality of our conversations with him.

I wish I could make that statement leap off the page, because what it contains is so important, and there are so many Christians who do not grasp this vital truth. So let me say it one more time.

Communion with God is a feast!

Thank You, God, for all You have given me. I love what You are doing in my heart, and I want You even more. Draw me ever deeper into this amazing relationship with You. In Jesus' name...

Personal Reflection

What is it worth to you to have a working relationship with God?

What would you need to do in order to arrange your life to make a space for these kinds of conversations?

Discussion Questions

What kinds of practical arrangements have you made in your life that have made it possible to find the time to talk with God?

What are some of the unique benefits you have experienced so far in your conversations with God?

Addendum

This addendum is intended to tie up a few loose ends and address some common questions about having conversations with God.

GOD SPEAKS!

Like many others, I grew up believing that God stopped talking as soon as the last few words of Revelation were penned by John, and that today God speaks only through his written Word. Since we do not have direct personal guidance, we must depend on various other ways of discerning God's leading in our lives – through principles found in the Bible, through the wise counsel of friends, and through specific circumstances that might confirm whatever it is we think God is trying to tell us. But apart from a few miraculous exceptions, the notion of direct communication was theologically unacceptable, even unthinkable.

Part of the rationale for this understanding was that if God spoke to us, we would have to call it "divine revelation" which by definition meant that it would be on par with the Bible. Since the Bible has clearly been completed, one must conclude that God no longer speaks. But that line of reasoning makes a number of unwarranted assumptions that we will address shortly.

Of course, there are some very *practical* reasons for not believing everyone can hear from God. For one thing, there are those who claim to hear from God but then lead people down all sorts of paths that have nothing whatever to do with God. Then there is the problem of people getting contradictory "revelations" that cannot all be from God. How does a person sort out who is telling the truth and who is confused or deliberately misleading? One might easily conclude that it would be better to hear nothing at all.

Why God Speaks to Us Personally

At first take, it might appear that we can solve a lot of problems by simply limiting God's word to what we find in the Bible. Unfortunately, this not only fails to solve the problems just stated, it introduces still more. If you will walk through this with me, I will give you eight very good reasons why these objections to hearing God really make very little sense.

To begin with, even among conservative scholars who agree on the basic principles of interpretation there exists a wide range of understanding on very fundamental issues.[13] Limiting God's voice to the written Word in no way ends the confusion about how to live the Christian life or when to do what.

Second, the Bible is primarily a collection of stories about people who were led by the Spirit or not led, written down to show us what a difference that makes. Paul tells us that we have those stories specifically to show us what we need to know about how to live.[14] *If then we have no direct means to be led by the Spirit, how are we to make any sense of those stories?* The one thing they do *not* tell us is how to live life without God's direct leading.

In fact, they often provide examples of how our best idea of what to do apart from God's voice falls short of what God has in

---

[13] One glaring example is Romans 7 where Paul exclaims, "O wretched man that I am!" Whether Paul is speaking about the Christian experience has *profound* implications for bondage and freedom for believers. Yet theologians are deeply divided over how to make sense of Paul's literary style and meaning.

[14] "Now these things happened to them as an example, and they were written for our instruction" (1Cor.10:11).

mind, such as when the disciples wanted to keep the children away from Jesus or send the crowds home, or when King Saul decided to do Samuel's job. Or consider how very different the story of Cornelius might be if God had not visited Peter prior to that encounter and given him the understanding he needed in order to renew his preconceived ideas about Gentiles. If anything, *these stories show us how utterly dependent we are upon the Spirit for navigating through life.*

Third, these stories make a lot of sense when we see that the level of discernment needed to live well is actually way beyond our ability. If God does not show us how to see and discern, then we are left to "our own understanding"[15] which is precisely what gets us into trouble in the first place!

A lot of Christians seem to think that if you are applying Biblical principles to your life then you are not leaning on your own understanding. But that is really rather naive. You are still relying on your powers of reason and judgment to decide not only what principles to apply in a given situation, but also (for example) *when* to be proactive in loving someone, *what kind* of love would be most appropriate for this one person at this time, and so on. We may feel very "scriptural" in our actions and yet be way off base in terms of what is truly needed or loving at the time.

To demonstrate how true this is, all we need to do is ask a simple question. How often have you looked back on something you did years earlier (even as a Christian) and wished you had known then what you know now? That should be evidence enough that it takes a lot more than good doctrine in order to live well. Because even when armed with doctrine we still have to rely "on our own understanding" in order to make the necessary judgment calls. On the other hand, instead of waiting for another

---

[15] "Trust in the Lord with all your heart and do not lean on your own understanding" (Prov.3:5).

ten years for our wisdom to grow, what if we could engage with our Mentor to ask for help? Then we would be relying on God's wisdom in regard to what to do.

Fourth, Jesus was very explicit about the ministry of the Holy Spirit as a mentor for life (Jn.16). As he was preparing his disciples for the end of his earthly ministry, Jesus carefully explained to them that his mission to train them was not over, and he was passing that task of mentoring on to the Holy Spirit. Given the context of his statements, there is no way that we could reasonably interpret those promises as a prophetic description of the Bible. The disciples still needed far too much personal attention to leave them with nothing more than their own best interpretation of inspired writings. And we today are as much in need of a mentor as they were.

Fifth, if the Bible is our only source of God's word to us, then one would have to say that for much of history the majority of his word was beyond reach for most Christians. That being the case, in what way does his promise to be with his people and guide them make any sense at all? Is Christianity a way of life that requires literacy or access to another literate person in order to grow? Did Christians need the invention of the printing press (around 1436) in order to begin to grow spiritually? These are not trivial problems. It may be easy to equate God's word to the printed text in modern times in modernized countries, but that perspective has serious implications for millions of Christians over many centuries who would have had no significant access to the truth necessary for life.

Sixth, Jesus addressed *this very issue* with the religious leaders of his day. Having no other direct source at the time, they were looking to the Scriptures for every detail on how to live. But Jesus argued that the purpose of the Scriptures was to point to Jesus himself, and that life was something that came from engaging with him, not something that could be extracted from the printed text alone.[16] How are we to make sense of this interchange if his intention was to point us back to the written Word as our only source on how to live?

Seventh, while the Bible is "living and active" we can see that it does not do its work automatically. People read the Bible all the time and walk away virtually unchanged. Nearly every Christian who has attempted a devotional life has gone through periods of time where reading the Bible seemed more like doing homework than feeding the soul, despite their best efforts. We can try to find ways to fault the person involved. Or we can consider the possibility that we need divine help in order to quicken the Word to our heart and mind, and that most of us have had little training on how to participate with the Holy Spirit in this way.

Finally, the Christian life is not just about knowing the right things to do. And knowing how to make good choices is not the only reason for having his Word. Our needs go way beyond correct answers about what to do. We need to be loved! We need to have a functional relationship with God.

As important and inherently full of life as the Scriptures are, we need God himself in order to live. God created us as relational creatures, he desires a relationship with us, and his directives are ultimately about being relational. That is why the two great commandments are to love God and love one another. He promised to be with us and guide us in all things, not just by giving us principles to live by, but by mentoring us in life and by speaking truth into our heart that we need day by day. And he was very careful to be quite explicit about this matter of listening to his voice.

---

[16] "You search the scriptures, because you think that in *them* you will find life. But the purpose of the scriptures is to point to the source of life, which is *me*." (Jn.5:39, paraphrased).

Just as *the manner* in which a person says something to us is as important as *what* they say, so hearing God speak things into our heart in exactly the way we need to hear them is part of what makes a conversational connection with him so life-giving. God's voice carries with it the power of life. His word is life, bread for the soul (Isa.55:1-3). And we need to receive directly from him in order to have life.

What the Bible Says About God Speaking

Here are just a few excerpts from the Bible declaring the truth that God speaks to us. Please note that these are not mere figures of speech referring to the Bible. They are clear descriptions of God's intention to speak directly into the lives of his people.

"Listen carefully to me, and eat what is good, and delight yourselves in rich food. Incline your ear, and come to me; listen so that you may live" (Isa.55:2-3).

"You shall not live by bread alone, but by every word that comes from the mouth of God" (Mt.4:4).

"I tell you the truth, a time is coming and has now come when the dead will hear the voice of the Son of God and those who hear will live" (Jn.5:25)

"The watchman opens the gate for him, and the sheep listen to his voice. He calls his own sheep by name and leads them out. When he has brought out all his own, he goes on ahead of them, and his sheep follow him because they know his voice ... My sheep listen to my voice; I know them, and they follow me" (Jn.10:3-5,27).

"The Spirit of truth who goes out from the Father, he will testify about me" (Jn.15:26).

"The Counselor, the Holy Spirit, whom the Father will send in my name, will teach you all things and will remind you of everything I have said to you" (Jn.14:26).

"I have much more to say to you, more than you can now bear. But when he, the Spirit of truth, comes, he will guide you into all truth. He will not speak on his own; he will speak only what he hears ... he will bring glory to me by taking from what is mine and making it known to you" (Jn.16:12-14).

Collectively, these verses tell us that God loves to teach, that we have much to learn, and that he wants to show us life as he sees it. Most of all, God speaks to us as part of being fully present with us and having a substantive relationship with us. What we need is help understanding *how* God speaks and how we can best hear what he is saying to us.

If God Speaks Today wouldn't that be considered revelation that is equal to scripture?

Understanding the tremendous difference between Scripture and personal revelation is very important. As background to this discussion, let us briefly review how the Bible came to be what it is today.

The Bible is not just one book with a single human author. There are sixty-six books, written by at least forty authors over a period of several centuries. But equally important, those books represent only a fraction of the total Jewish and Christian writings of that period of history, yet we ended up with only sixty-six of them. Why is that?

Long before the birth of Christ, Jewish scholars selected from their writings those which they believed had particular value for all

Jews everywhere. Similarly, there were a number of church councils in the first few centuries after Christ where they selected from among various Christian writings those which they believed were normative for everyone in the church at large.

Of course they had other criteria as well, but the main issue for our purposes here is that this unique collection of Judeo-Christian material was deemed important for all Christians in all places and all times. These collective works, sometimes referred to as *the canon of Scripture*, were eventually copied into a single volume which we now call the Bible. And we sometimes refer to the Bible as *General Revelation* because it is for everyone.

In contrast to that, when we are being tutored by the Spirit of God for our personal edification, the means and purposes are somewhat different. There God takes into account the unique circumstances of our life, our prior learning, the ways in which we have been shaped by experience, the people with whom we are currently connected, and any other resources we have at hand.

Within that context, he then crafts one-of-a-kind ways of revealing truth that we personally need for renewal. Revelations of this type are not meant to be adopted as normative experiences for all Christians everywhere. They are for our own edification only (though they may become instructive or inspirational for others who hear our story). And so we refer to this as *personal revelation*.

There are many examples of personal revelation in the Bible, included so we can follow along as those people were taught or directed by God. If we happen to learn something from what God revealed to them, that is alright, too. But his primary intent was to work with the person in the story as an example of how he works with all of us. We learn how to engage with God by listening in on their stories. Let's see how this plays out in a very well-known narrative.

In the Old Testament, David was confronted by God through the prophet Nathan in such a way as to reveal *David's condition* and *God's perspective* at the same time (2Sam.12). The illustration that Nathan used was tailored in just the right way to engage David's true heart, in which he cared about protecting and defending good people against abuses of power.

Once Nathan had David emotionally invested in the story, he moved the spotlight to David's previous actions, which brought him face to face with the seriousness of his betrayal of God and of his friend. Overwhelmed by what he had tried to hide from himself, David wept and sought out forgiveness for his sin.

Now we could try to distill some principles from this story about how self-centered lust can destroy lives or how no one is immune from making terrible mistakes. But those lessons are spelled out well enough in other places. Nathan's parable may have some usefulness for the people of God everywhere. But its real value was to reach David specifically in that moment of his life. What is truly normative for everyone in this story is how God can meet us so skillfully and reveal to us what we need in order to restore us to life, no matter how vile our past behavior.

When we view the story in this light, we can see a big difference between what is personal revelation and what is general revelation. And while this *particular* story of personal revelation was recorded in order to teach us some important truths, it would be unreasonable to assume that *all* personal revelation needs to be recorded for everyone to see.

I suppose we could all record our experiences of God and share them with each other. But there is no reason why we would need to equate those stories to scripture or confuse personal revelation with general revelation. Instead, we should rejoice that God can speak to his people today and offer them what they need for life.

WHAT ABOUT PEOPLE WHO "HEAR" CRAZY THINGS?

Having said all the things we did about God's protection from the enemy, we must acknowledge that there are people who "hear" some very crazy things and attribute them to God. In my experience, these anomalies can be divided into several groups.

First, there are those relatively few who are outright fabricators, whose character often gives them away. They seek personal glory or power and have little to no interest in becoming an instrument of grace. They can usually be identified by their overarching narcissism, ambition, or immaturity. In some cases what they really need is to be helped and mentored. But once in a while they need to be singled out as a danger to the larger group.

Then there are those people who want to justify their desire for something and therefore hear whatever it is they want to hear. In this way God can be used to "approve" unwise decisions such as a foolish marriage proposal, an extravagant lifestyle, a shady business deal, and a host of other things we might want to feel good about. Of course, we must be aware that discerning well can be a tricky thing when we are praying about things in which we have a vested interest in the outcome. In those cases we should seek out help from others who know how to discern well.

Two other areas where people hear strange things involve those who are very much in need of our prayers and support. One has to do with someone whose brain has been injured or is malfunctioning in some way. As stated earlier, our brain, mind and spirit are woven together in some mysterious ways in which each impacts the other. When our neurological circuits are not working the way they were designed, we can experience problems in our spiritual connections as well. The community of believers must be careful to hold such people in their hearts and if necessary be their spiritual eyes and ears for them.

Please notice that up to this point we are not talking about demonic influences. Even though people may not be hearing from God very well, there is nothing sinister necessarily at work here, and no thoughts from the enemy need be involved. People are mostly hearing their own thoughts.

So the last group we need to address are those who have been involved in the occult in some manner and have not yet received complete deliverance from whatever they were in alignment with previously. Having been opened up to evil in the past, they may have not yet received the deliverance necessary to seal off those avenues of access to their soul. Some measure of demonic oppression or dividedness within them may be preventing their full desire for God's leading or keeping them from trusting him to be different than what they have known before.

For those who fall into this category, it is extremely important that they work closely with other Christians who can hear well from God and have some experience in discerning the difference between God and enemy counterfeits. That way they will have some safeguards against being drawn away by more deception, as well as a way to be mentored in the discernment process.

Suggested Passages for Reflection and Journaling

As a way of jump-starting your conversations with God, I would suggest that you take each of the following passages, one at a time, and have at least one extended time of reflection and listening to see what God wants you to know about them.

"Blessed are the spiritually impoverished, because they get to be in the Kingdom too!" (Mt.5:3, paraphrase).

"Come to me, all you that are weary and are carrying heavy burdens, and I will give you rest. Take my yoke upon you, and learn from me; for I am gentle and humble in heart, and you will find rest for your souls. For my yoke is easy, and my burden is light" (Mt.11:28-30).

Consider how much Mary and Elizabeth needed each other and why (Lk.1:39-56).

"For he himself is kind to the ungrateful and the wicked. Be merciful, just as your Father is merciful" (Lk.6:35-36).

Parable of the Prodigal Sons (Lk.15:11-32). This story is full of possibilities.

"If you only knew the gift of God and who it was speaking to you" (Jn.4:10).

"And those who love me will be loved by my Father, and I will love them and reveal myself to them ... we will come to them and make our home with them" (Jn.14:21,23).

"Peace I leave with you; my peace I give to you. I do not give to you as the world gives" (Jn.14:27).

"You did not choose me but I chose you. And I appointed you to go and bear fruit, fruit that will last" (Jn.15:16). Compare this to Ps.1:3.

"He who did not withhold his own Son, but gave him up for all of us, will he not with him also give us everything else?" (Rom.8:32).

"Do you not know that your body is a temple of the Holy Spirit within you, which you have from God, and that you are not your own? For you were bought with a price" (Rom.6:19-20).

"But we have this treasure in clay jars" (2Cor.4:7).

"We look not at what can be seen but at what cannot be seen ... we walk by faith, not by sight" (2Cor.4:18; 5:7).

"I have been crucified with Christ; and it is no longer I who live, but it is Christ who lives in me. And the life I now live in the flesh I live by faith in the Son of God, who loved me and gave himself for me" (Gal.2:19-20).

"Until Christ is formed in you" (Gal.4:19).

"Blessed with every spiritual blessing in the heavenly places" (Eph.1:3).

Ponder the massive work of God toward us presented in Eph.1:3-14.

Reflect on various elements of Paul's prayer in Eph.1:17-20.

"But God, who is rich in mercy, out of the great love with which he loved us even when we were dead" (Eph.2:4-5).

"For we are what he has made us, created in Christ Jesus for good works, which God prepared beforehand *to be our way of life*" (Eph.2:10).

Ponder various elements of Paul's prayer in Eph.3:16-19.

"Abundantly far more than all we can ask or imagine" (Eph.3:20).

"The whole body, joined and knit together by every ligament with which it is equipped, as each part is working properly, promotes the body's growth in building itself up in love" (Eph.4:16).

"That your love may overflow more and more with knowledge and full insight" (Phil.1:9).

"The surpassing value of knowing Christ Jesus my Lord" (Phil.3:8).

"To be found in him" (Phil.3:9).

"Becoming like him" (Phil.3:10).

"Having righteousness that comes from God by faith [not by self-effort]" (Phil.3:8-10).

Consider various elements of Paul's prayer in Col.1:9-13.

"For he has rescued us from the power of darkness and transferred us into the Kingdom of his beloved Son" (Col.1:13).

"Christ in you, the hope of glory" (Col.1:27).

"So they may have all the riches of assured understanding and have the knowledge of God's mystery, that is, Christ himself, in whom are hidden all the treasures of wisdom and knowledge" (Col.2:2). Slow this down and look at the implications of having Christ in you – HE is our source, not our ability to acquire knowledge or do things.

"God made you alive together with him" (Col.2:13).

"You have died, and your life is hidden with Christ in God" (Col.3:3).

"Seek those things which are above ... set your mind on things that are above, not on things that are on the earth" (Col.3:1-2).

"You have put on the new self, *which is being renewed*" (Col.3:10).

"To those who reside as *aliens*" (1Pet.1:1).

"Whose divine power has given us everything needed for life and godliness through knowing him" (2Pet.1:3).

This is what John learned from all of his time with Jesus: "God is light – in Him is no darkness at all" (1Jn.1:5).

"See what love the Father has given us, that we should be called children of God; and that is what we are" (1Jn.3:1).

"There is no fear in love, but perfect love casts out fear" (1Jn.4:18). Reflect on what Trust has to do with fear and love.

"Hey, everyone who thirsts. And you that have no money. Come, buy and eat. Come buy wine and milk without money and without cost ... Listen, listen to me, and eat what is good, and your soul will delight in the richest of fare. Incline your ear and come to me; listen, that your soul may live" (Isa.55:1-3).

"One thing I ask of the LORD, this is what I seek: that I may dwell in the house of the LORD all the days of my life, to gaze upon the beauty of the LORD and to seek him in his temple" (Ps.27:4).

"How lovely is your dwelling place, O LORD Almighty! My soul yearns, even faints, for the courts of the LORD; my heart and my flesh cry out for the living God" (Ps.84:1-2).

Also consider reading through these entire chapters, verse-by-verse:

Isaiah 55, Psalms 23, 27, 84, 100, and 139
John 14-17, Ephesians 1-4, and Colossians 1-3.

RESOURCES FOR FURTHER STUDY

Dallas Willard: *Hearing God: Developing a Conversational Relationship With God* (1984)
>Provides a strong theological basis for listening to God in the present day, describes what it is like to hear God's voice, and discusses various issues surrounding this topic.
>Available on Amazon.com.

Jan Johnson: *When the Soul Listens* (1999)
>A wonderful invitation to contemplative prayer. Jan's style and stories very effectively draw the reader into wanting a stronger relationship with God. The book continues to grow in depth as you read. See www.JanJohnson.org.

David Takle: *The Truth About Lies And Lies About Truth* (2008)
>An in-depth look at how God changes lives though engaging with him for truth. See: www.TruthAboutLies.info.

Live Demonstrations
For many people, listening to the Spirit only begins to make sense when they see someone else engage with God. Sometime during 2011 we hope to begin recording some conversations with God on video and making them available for viewing. Please check the following websites for these resources.

Listen.LifeModel.org
or
Listen.KingdomFormation.org

Other Sources Cited

Benner, David: *Desiring God's Will: Aligning Our Hearts with the Heart of God* (Intervarsity Press: Downers Grove) 2005

Fee, Gordon and Stuart, Douglas: *How to Read the Bible for All Its Worth* (Zondervan: Grand Rapids) 1981

Edman, V. Raymond: *They Found the Secret: 20 Transformed Lives That Reveal a Touch of Eternity* (Zondervan: Grand Rapids) 1960, 1984

Lewis, C. S.: *The Lion, the Witch, and the Wardrobe* (HarperColins: New York) 1994

Smith, James Bryan: *The Good and Beautiful God: Falling in Love with the God Jesus Knows* (Intervarsity Press: Downers Grove) 2009

Wilder, E. James and Coursey, Chris: *Share Immanuel: The Healing Lifestyle*, (Shepherd's House: Pasadena) 2010

Wilder, Jim and Khouri, Ed: *Belonging* (Shepherd's House: Pasadena) 2011 (see Resources.LifeModel.org)

For more help understanding the power of relationship to shape our mind and our life, see www.LifeModel.org and the various resources there.

Made in the USA
Charleston, SC
19 July 2011